CHOSEN: Black America's Calling

Brooks B. Robinson, Ph.D.

The Cover

Because the Black American experience has produced a people who physically reflect all of mankind's hues, we propose that a new Black American nation select as its flag colors that represent all of man's hues. By so doing, we reflect respect for all humans—red, yellow, black, brown, tan, and white.

Dedication

For past and present Black American males who desired to change the course of Black American history, but could not.

Preface

Welcome again to another invitation to Black Americans to accept their special challenge at this critical juncture in global history and form their own nation. *Choice: Black America's Decision* initiated this invitation by building on efforts that extend back to the 19th century to move Black Americans toward founding their own nation. That initial effort may not have been convincing because it may have lacked sufficient context. This book, *CHOSEN: Black America's Calling*, adds significantly more context.

While nation formation may not happen suddenly, it may and can happen more quickly than we might anticipate. World developments during the 21st century are rapid-paced. Therefore, it is imperative that Black Americans begin to form their decision about taking appropriate actions that will produce a new nation and bring considerably enhanced well-being and happiness.

A popular song in today's Gospel *genre* is "God's Got a Blessing with Your Name on It." What greater blessing could be forthcoming for Black Americans than their own nation with the opportunity to control their destiny under the guidance of the Almighty?

We hope to live to see this reality. If we don't in our current physical form, then we believe that we will be present in spirit. What we know is that God's word has been spoken on this matter, and that His word is TRUE! "Let's get back to Eden and live on top of the world."

Foreword

Some may find this book to be out of the realm of economics—at least initially. They may come to this conclusion because it discusses religious and historical issues in advance of coming to seemingly economic concerns. The reality is that the world is fastly recognizing that the entire purpose of economics is to create circumstances under which quality of life, otherwise known as well-being, is enhanced. Therefore, if economists are to remain relevant, then they must find themselves searching for ways to assist economic agents in improving their quality of life.

This book contains three independent essays that are intended to open a window on to nation formation for Black Americans. First, it explains the false underpinnings of current Judeo-Christian traditions using Islamic traditions as a counter-balance. Second, it explains conditions that Black Americans are likely to face in the future that will make it imperative for them to exodus the United States. Third, it provides a draft blueprint for Black Americans to use to fulfill their purpose in the 21st century. Essentially, the book contends that Black Americans have been *CHOSEN* to perform a special set of tasks on the world stage in the period ahead.

Will Black Americans prove God to be a liar or prove God to be true, who has all power in his mouth and in his hand? That is the key question that we establish in this book. Of course, Black Americans have a choice in shaping their answer to this question.

CHOSEN should enable Black Americans to see that, by making the correct choice, they choose a path for improving their well-being and for setting a standard that can produce improved outcomes for the remainder of the world.

Either Black Americans will not make the correct choice and fall into oblivion, or they will choose God, his truth, and enhanced well-being for themselves and for the rest of the world. If our earlier book, *Choice: Black America's Decision,* was insufficient to motivate Black Americans to move down the road toward nation formation, then, hopefully, *CHOSEN: Black America's Calling* will.

Table of Contents

Introduction

Black America has spent the first decade of the 21st century grappling with the idea that the world has changed. The revolution in information technology that characterized the last half of the final decade of the 20th century, the rise of Asia as an economic power during the first decade of the current century, and American firms' decision to export innumerable jobs abroad, have created a new economic paradigm in the United States (U.S.). That paradigm reflects fewer relatively high-paying manufacturing jobs, and an abundance of relatively lower-paying jobs in service industries. These changes are not likely to be reversed in the near term. Moreover, the global financial and economic crises of 2008-9, which had their seeds in the 9/11 experience, weakened the U.S. economy to the brink of collapse.

The depth, breadth, and scope of the financial crisis, the increase in government borrowing to finance economic stimulus and assistance programs, and the funds required to fight wars in Iraq and Afghanistan, have placed the U.S. government under a severe fiscal strain. State and local governments are also not immune to the economic doldrums. Ultimately, these conditions and the action that the Federal Reserve Board has taken to counteract them will drive up interest rates and increase inflation. In the aftermath of higher interest rates and inflation, certain experts believe that the U.S. economy will experience the type of very weak conditions that parallel those experienced by Japan during the last two "lost" decades.

Given an underlying tone of White supremacy in the U.S., White Americans are feeling more and more put out by the fact that they can no longer count on finding a well-paying job. If the principle of hysteresis holds, workers will continue to look for such jobs and find that they do not exist. When White Americans look around and see that certain Blacks have jobs, while they do not, then this will motivate great consternation. Malcolm X (a.k.a. el-Hajj Malik el-Shabazz) said that, "the surest way to start a bloody race war is to take a job from a White and give it to a Black."[1] Therefore, Black Americans must realize that their precarious state in the U.S. could become even more precarious.

Most importantly, Black Americans should realize that the election of a Black American to the position of President of the U.S. does not mean that conditions will improve for them. In fact, we believe that history will reveal that Mr. Obama's success was designed to distract Black Americans from the task that should have occupied their attention at this juncture in history—founding their own new nation.

---

[1] This quote is from a Malcolm X's speech entitled, "The End of White World Supremacy," (circa 1960).

Given all of the foregoing, Black Americans should recognize that it is in their long-term best interest to begin to seek to found their own nation. If they do not, then they will inevitably and perpetually be engaged in efforts to mitigate physical and economic crises that they will confront. Black Americans are now a nation within a nation that needs to find its own home, move out, and grow up. If not, then that nation's growth will be stunted forever. Unless they take such action, they will be forever looked upon as a people who were too weak minded and unwilling to do for themselves.

But the stigma will be even more pernicious because Black Americans have been shaped to play a very select and special role in the world during this millennium. If they fail to mature and fulfill that role, then the world itself is subject to crises that may go unresolved. When the world realizes that Black Americans could have saved the world but didn't, then Black Americans will be stigmatized forever.

CHOSEN attempts to crystallize the foregoing scenario and to assist Black Americans in seeing the clear path to nation formation. Black Americans have always looked for opportunity, they have always yearned for the big meeting, and they have always wanted to show the world what they are capable of accomplishing by the will and grace of God. Now they have an opportunity to form a nation, they can gather in that nation until their hearts are content, and they can show the world their nation-building skills.

The last great movement in the United States by Black Americans during the 1960s ended with little direction from leadership on how to proceed. After a four-decade-long pause during which Black Americans have had an opportunity to reshape and grow their ideologies, it is now time to initiate a new movement that will result in nation formation. Black Americans should not fear the complexity or difficulty of the task, but they should meet the challenge head on. They can rest assured that their efforts will be successful because "it is written," and because they are the *CHOSEN*.

Essay 1: Hebrews/Jews and Black Americans

Summary: This essay discusses the role of a "chosen people of God" in the context of world history. It highlights claims by those known in today's world as "Hebrews" or "Jews," and explains that Black Americans are the people who best fit spiritual prophesy concerning a chosen people of God in the current era. It notes that an almighty God will not be frustrated, and that those who call themselves Jews today, through their actions, represent a people who would frustrate God—if he could be frustrated. On the other hand, Black Americans have been the lambs of the world who have survived even though they have been open prey to the world's wolves. In the end, God's word must be true and Black Americans serve as that people who have worshiped God and Him alone. His praise is eternally in their mouths. Finally, Black Americans are blessed and shall be blessed (economically and otherwise) because they neither cursed their God nor sought death. On the contrary, Black Americans have survived against all odds in order to, in fact, show the world that God is God and that beside him there is no other. Black Americans are living proof that God can make something out of nothing.

Introduction

Judeo-Christian-Islamic traditions constitute the fundamental principles that undergird a considerable proportion of world societies. The given order of those traditions is instructive; you cannot have one without the other and in the order described. What is problematic about the order of the traditions, the principles, and the societies is that they are built on falsehood. There are at least two key principles that sit at the seat of the falsehood. One is that so-called Hebrews are the "chosen people of God." The second is that European Christians permitted "White Supremacy" as a concept to find root in their religion, and that they used that concept to manipulate the world exclusively to their advantage.

We will use the next few pages to explain basic falsehoods that underlay the traditions; revelation of those falsehoods, in turn, uproots White Supremacy. This process will evolve with references to both religious and economic concepts and principles. While our formal training is in economics, revelations about falsehoods in the religious traditions come from a life-long interest and informal study of religious traditions. We claim no particular expertise in these fields (economics or religion); however, we believe that it does not take great expertise to uncover the concerns that we discuss. What is required is a willingness to read carefully the literature and to seek clarity. It was this process that enables us to share the following insights with you.

Falsehoods in the Hebrew/Jewish Tradition

Given that we are not scholars of the Hebrew language, we cannot say that we have read the *Taurat* as it is now configured. But that may not be problematic because, unlike the Islamic tradition, today's Jews cannot claim that their current religious text is pure and complete; i.e., in its original form. The New Oxford Annotated Bible (1973) contains a long analysis of the various versions of the *Old Testament* and *New Testaments*. It becomes clear quickly that the Hebrews/Jews lost the writings given to Moses, and that many of the books that constitute the current Christian *Old Testament* were lost and reconstructed over the centuries. Consequently, there must undoubtedly be much uncertainty about the veracity of what is now recorded in the current *Taurat* and, by extension, the *Old Testament.*

Jewish scholars are likely to take issue with the idea that we are discussing the *Taurat* and the *Old Testament* in the same breath. If they take issue with this analysis, and if they can identify great discrepancies between the *Taurat* and the relevant books from the *Old Testament*, then we invite them to step forward and correct us. But they should also correct their Christian brethren—showing them the error of their ways. Most Christians believe that, as applicable, the *Old Testament* and the *Taurat* are consistent. If they are not, then Christians might change their perception of Christianity if they were to be fully informed concerning those differences. In other words, this book offers an opportunity for Jews to open up their *Taurat* to the world and to clarify what differences exist between their book and what Christians are studying in their monasteries, seminaries, and churches.

It is not necessary to identify every falsehood that is embedded in today's *Taurat* and *Old Testament*. If basic falsehoods can be identified, then those will be sufficient to render questionable the remainder of the book. Of course, it is not usually appropriate to throw out the baby with the bathwater; however, if the bathwater is dirty, then the baby will not be clean. That is not to say that Jews should fully discount their religion once they hear about the inaccuracies that are inherent in their book. However, a word to the wise should be sufficient. That is to say that identification of inconsistencies in the *Taurat* should motivate Jews to perform a further search for the truth, make efforts to correct their book (assuming that they desire to be righteous), and then to transform their lives, living, and religion to be consistent with truth.

We plan to discuss only a few falsehoods that are inherent in the *Taurat* and the *Old Testament*. One falsehood concerns Abraham and his progeny. The second involves the historical veracity of a 430-year-long sojourn of Hebrews in Egypt as slaves. The third concerns unrighteous elements of the Hebrew tradition, the *Taurat*, and, thereby, related books in the *Old Testament*. In other words, we question whether an all knowing, all wise, benevolent, and merciful God would form a covenant with a people like the people portrayed in the *Old Testament*, whose lives were filled with lies, treachery, and deceit. Most importantly, we ask whether God would ever single out only one group or people with which to form a special relationship—effectively excluding other groups and people from his love, mercy, and grace.

Abraham and His Progeny

Judaism rests on Abraham (initially Abram)—the father of the religion, whose god becomes the God of Israel. In the book of *Genesis* (Chapters 12-25), it is recorded that, initially, Abraham's wife Sarah (initially Sarai) was unable to conceive. Consequently, Sarah gave her maid servant, Hagar, to Abraham to produce a child on Sarah's behalf. Abraham and Hagar's union produced a son, Ishmael—Abraham's first born son. Abraham's God blesses Ishmael and indicates that his seed shall prosper and produce a great nation through the course of time (*Genesis* 16:10). Today we know that Ishmael is the father of the Arab nations.

Sarah becomes jealous of Hagar and distraught after Ishmael's birth. So much so that she commands

Abraham to send Hagar and Ishmael away. Hagar and Ishmael become stranded in the desert— according to Islamic tradition, at the *Zam-Zam well* and between the hills of *Safa* and *Marwa*. It is at this location that Hagar cries out to Abraham's God for help, and God responds by miraculously providing nourishment and reveals the presence of the *Zam-Zam* well (*Genesis* 21:9-21). This miracle saves Hagar and Ishmael's lives, and enables them to be reunited with Abraham and Sarah at a later point.

These biblical passages make plain the fact that Ishmael is Abraham's first born son. In the tradition of the day, then, Ishmael would possess primogenitor rights; i.e., the son with the right to receive the bulk of his father's estate and, at the point of his father's death, his father's blessing.

It turns out that God works a miracle with Sarah and enables her to conceive and bear a son for Abraham, Isaac, who extends Abraham lineage to the people who were to come to call themselves Hebrews and Jews. Isaac, too, is blessed by Abraham's God and is said to be the origin of a great nation (*Genesis* 22:17). Genesis goes on to report that, at the point of Abraham's death, Isaac receives Abraham's estate and his blessing.

What is befuddling about the record in *Genesis* is that it clearly reports that Ishmael is Abraham's first born and that he is blessed by God, but that it does not then provide a clear explanation for why Ishmael does not receive the traditional honors that accompany primogenitorship. In fact, the *Genesis* records a blatant lie in this regard when it reports that Isaac is Abraham's "only son" at the point when Abraham is asked to perform a sacrifice to God (see *Genesis* 22:2, 22:12, and 22:16).[2] This language appears to be purposeful and it makes clear the point that it is critical that Isaac be recognized as Abraham's only son in order to sidestep primogenitor conventions and to, thereby, create a clear path for the nation of Israel to be born as a special people.

Later in *Genesis*, we find other cases where second sons are favored over first sons due to trickery and intentionally.[3] Nevertheless, these cases are viewed as anomalies because the law of primogenitorship is so entrenched. Moreover, there is no convincing or sufficient argument to explain why Abraham "had" to produce his first son through Sarah. A broad reading of the *Genesis*, presumably the *Taurat*, and the *Old Testament* is that God is dealing most extensively with males and works through females to a much

---

[2] Notably, biblical and Qur'anic differences extend to Abraham's sacrifice of his son. The *Holy Bible* records the sacrificial son as Isaac (*Genesis* 22:9-10), while the *Holy Qur'an* infers that the sacrificial son was Ishmael (*Holy Qur'an* 19:54).

[3] There are two notable cases where the law of primogenitor is violated. The first case involves Isaac's sons Esau and Jacob; the latter wins his father's blessing by trickery with help from his mother (*Genesis* 27:1-29). The second case involves Joseph's two oldest sons; at the point of death, Israel blesses Joseph's second son—not his first son (*Genesis* 48:5-20).

lesser extent. Therefore, it seems that it should be sufficient for Abraham to be holy in order for Ishmael to be holy and serve as primogenitor—irrespective of whether his mother was a hand maiden and a Black woman (a woman from Egypt). It does not go unnoticed that Jewish descent is determined through the mother not the father—even though Jews claim their God through their fathers: Abraham, Isaac, and Jacob.

Interestingly, *Genesis* records that Ishmael and Isaac grow up and collaborate on burying their father Abraham, but go their separate ways thereafter.[4] Once the split occurs, Ishmael descendants become outsiders to the Hebrews. It is instructive to recognize that, in many ways, Ishmael's seed has been more blessed than Isaac's seed. Even today, Arab nations continue to be the beneficiaries of their oil, and they have no history of Diaspora and Holocaust, which the Jews were unfortunate to have experienced.

The Veracity of the 430-Year Sojourn

In analyzing Judaism we must remember that, according to the *Old Testament*, the people that came to be called Jews (the Children of Israel) did not exist as a nation of people until after their sojourn in, and exodus from, Egypt. If the link between Egypt and the Hebrews is severed, then, theoretically, Jews never came into existence and do not exist today. It is

---

[4] See *Genesis* 25:9-18.

informative to learn today that great energy is being expended by scholars all over the world, but particularly by Jewish scholars, who seek to prove that the Hebrews were in Egypt. The reality is that there is no available irrefutable evidence that the biblical Hebrews were ever in Egypt.[5,6,7]

This lack of evidence is quite perplexing. The ancient Egyptian civilization was very advanced in writing, medicine, architecture, etc. Consequently, it is anomalous that there is little evidence in Egyptian History concerning the great Hebrew economist

---

[5] In 2006, the History Channel broadcast a documentary, "Exodus Decoded," concerning the efforts by Jewish scholars to prove that Jews were in Egypt. Their most potent evidence were ancient paintings of a scene of travelers wearing colorful coats (Joseph's coat of many colors); one or a few ring insignia's that purportedly represented a "Joseph stamp," which was supposedly related to Joseph's rule of the store houses of Egypt and his authority to manage the economy; and inscriptions on a cave wall that are interpreted to mean "God, save us from these mines," which includes an ancient rendering of the Hebrew word for God (Elohim) (see http://en.wikipedia.org/wiki/Exodus_Decoded).

[6] Kratovac (2010) writes in "Egypt: New Find Shows Slaves Didn't Build Pyramids" that, contrary to popular beliefs, the Hebrews were not in Egypt to build the pyramids. This article from the Associated Press confirms that the builders of the pyramids were the Egyptians themselves. But if the Hebrews were not under hard task masters in Egypt, then references to such conditions in *Genesis* and *Exodus* are false—meaning that the *Holy Bible* is inaccurate.

[7] Malcolm X (circa 1960), on the authority of the Honorable Elijah Muhammad, taught that the biblical personality known as Moses rescued a genetically engineered race of Whites from the caves of Europe, not from Egypt, and assisted them in their rise to form civilization.

Joseph, son of (Jacob), of the arrival of Joseph's family, and most importantly, of the departure of the great mass of Hebrews that constituted an exodus. It is quite odd that none of these events is clearly recorded in the Egyptian record, especially given that the Hebrews appear to have such a clear record of how these events transpired—at least as reflected in the *Old Testament*.

Clearly, while it is possible to "fool some of the people some of the time," in order to be convincing, usually, it is not wise to construct a history that includes bald-faced lies. Therefore, it may be the case that a tenuous link exists between Egypt and the Hebrews. However, that link may not be related to an actual 430-year sojourn in Egypt and an exodus.

What we must realize is that the link between Egypt and the biblical Hebrews is not the only aspect of Jewish History that is viewed as questionable by scholars. This book is not designed to provide a full accounting of research on the veracity of Jewish History. However, we want to call clearly into question the link between the Hebrews and Egypt. A recent and more systematic inquiry into the truth of Jewish History is a 2009 book by a Professor at Tel Aviv University in Israel, Shlomo Sand (the book is translated into English by Yael Lotan). The book is entitled *The Invention of the Jewish People*, which Prof. Sands uses to refute Jewish claims to the land that the State of Israel now occupies. Many such books have been written over the course of time, and more such books are likely to be written in the future. However, the fact that they are being written is further *prima facie* evidence that there is a dearth of actual historical evidence that substantiates the biblical history of the Hebrews.

It is ironic that the *Holy Bible*, in fact, contains its own evidence that the Hebrews were not in Egypt as slaves. In the *New Testament* book of *St. John* (8:33), the Jews are cited as telling Jesus, "We have never been in bondage to anyone." If this is viewed as a categorical statement, then one can conclude that the Hebrews were never in Egypt. On the other hand, if one does not accept the *Old Testament* account of Jewish History, why should one accept *New Testament* commentary on that history?

Given the lack of physical historical evidence concerning the biblical Hebrews being in Egypt, given the many literary works that have called into question various aspects of Jewish History, and given the *New Testament* proclamation concerning the Jews never being in bondage, we conclude that we are warranted in questioning the veracity of the biblical story concerning the Hebrew sojourn in, and exodus, from Egypt. The available evidence leads us to the realization that the biblical story of the Hebrews lacks veracity from an historical perspective.

Are Lies and Deceit Consistent with Righteousness?

Given our understanding of philosophy, religion, and God, it does not appear that Hebrews have a history or a tradition of righteousness. Why was their kingdom split? Why were they exiled? Why was the great temple destroyed twice? Why the centuries of disdain in Europe, which culminated in the horrific Jewish Holocaust (the veracity of which, too, has been questioned)? What we know about God is that he is oft forgiving and most merciful. Therefore, it seems unbelievable that God would suffer his chosen people to suffer so often for so long.

Now let's go further and take just the first book of the *Old Testament* and look at the nature of the Hebrew spirit. We will let you read the surrounding passages, but we would like to highlight what appears to be behavior that is antithetical to righteousness that the Hebrews performed and present plainly in their religious texts. All of these unrighteous acts are from *Genesis*, but there are many other such acts throughout the remainder of the *Old Testament:*

- Abraham lying about his relationship with his wife—saying to men that she was his sister (*Genesis* 12:13 and 20:2). If he was under God's protection, then why would he lie out of fear?

- Sarah lying to the angels that she did not laugh after having laughed upon hearing that she would bear a child at an advanced age (*Genesis* 18:15).
- Lot's daughters conceiving with him (*Genesis* 19:33-36). If they were taught to rely and trust God, would they have taken matters into their own hand?
- While primogenitor seems to hold sway throughout history, it is clearly abandoned when it comes to Abraham. Ishmael is not granted the benefits of primogenitorship. His brother Isaac is extended that benefit, even though he was Abraham's second son (*Genesis* 21:12). This conveniently sets up Isaac's line as the one granted "chosen" status.
- Jacob's crude strategy to extract Esau's birthright in exchange for porridge, as opposed to extending a good meal to his brother (*Genesis 25:29-34*).
- Jacob and his mother's efforts to co-opt Esau's birthright blessing from Isaac (*Genesis* 27:1-40*).
- Joseph's efforts to suck dry the entire Egyptian society's money, land, and cattle wealth during a drought on behalf of the Pharaoh—all except for priests (*Genesis* 47:13-26). Why was it favorable to break the populace and enrich Pharaoh?

These seven examples of lies, treachery, and deceit epitomize the cruel, crooked, and twisted nature of selected individuals in the Hebrew tradition. The unfortunate aspect of it all is that the more wicked (from a moral perspective) the act, the higher the praise of the related personality by Hebrews/Jews down through the course of history.

Who Are the Chosen People of God?

A people's religion is their religion. There is little that anyone can do, or should do, about that. Given human nature, it is expected that a people will develop a god and a religion that produce optimal well-being for them and their posterity. However, when a people develop a religion that includes claims that impact directly the remainder of the world's populace, then it is important to question the veracity of those claims.

Not being historians, we cannot state categorically that the claims of Hebrews/Jews have not been challenged sufficiently. What we do know is that Black Americans have not challenged sufficiently claims made by Jews. What important Jewish religious claims have Black Americans failed to challenge sufficiently? Actually, there are many claims that could be challenged, but it is critical that one key claim be challenged because the remaining questionable claims stem from it. The claim in question is that Hebrews/Jews are the "chosen people of God."

The reason why this claim should be challenged by Black Americans is two-fold. First, Black Americans are the product of a set of experiences that are very similar to the written text of a significant portion of the beginning section of the *Old Testament*. Second, as noted above, scholars are unable to substantiate as historical fact much of what is written in the early portions of the *Old Testament*, which relate the conditions under which Hebrews/Jews justify their claim to the "chosen" status.

Let us set aside, for a moment, the question of the actual veracity of the Hebrew claim of a sojourn in Egypt. Assuming that they were in Egypt for 430 years and then came out with great substance, what else should Black Americans challenge? For certain, Black Americans should not question the history that is revealed in the *Old Testament*. What Black Americans should challenge is the content of the *Old Testament*, and how that work results in the inference that Hebrews were selected by God as his chosen people. Let's begin with the latter before addressing the former.

First, we should be aware that the Egyptian King Amenhotep IV (a.k.a. Ikhnaton), before the time when the Hebrews supposedly departed Egypt, brought to light the concept of the one god (Williams, 1987; p.

110). In fact, religious experts can draw very close parallels between many aspects of Egyptian religion and the Hebrew religion. Therefore, assuming that Jews were in Egypt, they essentially co-opted several Egyptian traditions and incorporated them into their religion.

Second, going back to the "chosen people" claim, it does not ring true. Black American Islamic leader, Imam W.D. Muhammad, taught that if one wants to discern the veracity of a "thing," then consult creation. If the "thing" that you are questioning can be identified with some regularity in creation (the natural order of things), then that "thing" is likely to be valid. If not, then the "thing" is likely false. We can apply this principle in the case of the "chosen people" claim. We must acknowledge that, as do the Jews, the Supreme Being created the creation. The precise details of how this great feat was achieved are beyond our comprehension at this point. What we know about this creation is that it is based on a set of laws and principles. The creation operates according to these laws and principle. There are very few exceptions to the laws of creation. Yet God appears to have the creation proceed according to an almost chaotic pattern. But the creation does not convey, in all of its scope, breadth, and beauty, favoritism. Are there special cases of apes or orangutans? Are there special classes of dogs or cats? Are there special types of winds other than that some are stronger than others? Are there special rains other than that some are more intense than others? Are there special viruses other than that some mutate more rapidly than others? Are there special classes of ponds, lakes, streams, rivers, and oceans? Some of these water bodies are larger than others, some flow north while others flow south, some flow more rapidly and possess more volume than others, and some are fresh water, while others are salty. However, in the grand scheme of things, water is water. Is there a particular temperature other than that some or hotter and some or colder? Therefore, we have great difficulty looking into creation and identifying situations where God, the Creator, has singled out some aspect of his creation and inured to it some special privilege or advantage. Man himself, who some say is close in nature to other primates, may be singled out as having been granted special gifts. But each day, scientists find that man, in his natural state, is really not that different from his primate brothers. But even if man were a special creation (a little lower than the angels), would God then take the time to single out even a small group of men as the beneficiaries of a special status?

Conclusion

It is reasonable to believe that God permits his creation to evolve in stages, and that groups of people are granted an opportunity to serve in a unique capacity during specific periods of time. That is why world history records separately the Great

Vedic Civilization, Egyptian Civilization, the Greeks, the Romans, the Aztecs, the Mayans, and the Islamic Eras. But none of these people ever claimed to be "God's chosen" for all times.

In our view, the fact that Hebrews have been able to maintain some degree of continuity of their lineage over an extended period of time, and given that they have had the facility of writing for much of their claimed existence, they have been able to attempt to optimize their people's well-being by sending forth and standing on a "chosen people" claim for over 2500 years.

If they are a chosen people, then we must ask questions about the nature of these people. Does there history infer directly or indirectly that they are living under the protection and blessing of God? Not in our opinion. If the argument is that God loves the Jews despite their wrong doing, it does not appear that God's love has shielded them from pain and suffering.

There are Christians who say that the *New Testament* renders the *Old Testament* moot. They say that during the *Old Testament* era, God's people (the Jews) were "under the law," while during the *New Testament* age, God's people (all those (Jews and Gentiles) who accept Jesus Christ as their savior) are "under grace." Our response is that a close reading of the *Holy Bible* (*James* 1:17) reveals God's word saying that he "does not change." Therefore, it is difficult to rationalize how the "under the law" and "under grace" regimes reflect a God who does not change. In our view, the *Holy Bible* contains inconsistencies and pieces that do not fit.

Given all of the foregoing, it is difficult to conclude that Hebrews/Jews are the "chosen people of God"—especially in the current era. Their claim is problematic because it clouds the world view when another group of people must enter the stage to play a significant role in moving the world forward through a new phase of development. Specifically, the continuing claim of "chosen people" status by Jews hampers Black American's recognition of their own experience as a special experience that is being reward by God's beneficence, mercy, and karmic laws for all that they have endured. For Black Americans to shine brightly on the world stage and to perform the important tasks that they have been ordained to perform, Hebrews should discontinue blocking the world view with their false "chosen people of God" claim.

References

Kratovac, K. (2010). "Egypt: New Find Shows Slaves Didn't Build Pyramids." *Yahoo News.* January 11, 2010; retrieved from the Internet on January 17, 2010; http://news.yahoo.com/s/ap/20100111/ap_on_re_mi_ea/ml_egypt_antiquities/print .

Malcolm X. (circa 1960) . "The End of White World Supremacy." A recording of this speech was obtained from the George Mason University Library in the mid-1990s.

The Holy Bible. (1973). The New Oxford Annotated Bible. (H.G. May and B.M. Metzger, Editors.) Oxford University Press. New York, NY.

The Holy Qur'an. (1410 (1988/9)). English Translation of the Meaning and Commentary by Mushaf Al-Madinah An-Nabawiyah. King Fahd *Holy Qur'an* Printing Complex. Al-Madinah Al-Munawarah, Saudi Arabia.

Sand, S. (2009). *The Invention of the Jewish People.* Verso Books. Brooklyn, NY. (Translated into English by Yael Lotan)

Williams, C. (1987). *The Destruction of Black Civilization: Great Issues of Race from 4500 B.C. to 2000 A.D.* Third World Press. Chicago, IL.

Excerpt from Martin Luther King's "Mountain Top" Speech

Before proceeding to Essay 2, please take a moment to listen to the following audio recording of an excerpt from Martin Luther King's final speech. Please click on the following link: http://www.blackeconomics.org/Quickstart/AudioLib/MLKMT.mp3.

(This recording was downloaded from YouTube.com.)

Martin Luther King said:

> "...We've got some difficult days ahead . But it really doesn't matter with me now; because I've been to the mountain top. And I don't mind. Like anybody. I'd like to live a long life, Longevity has its place. But I'm not concerned about that now. I just want to do God's will. And he has allowed me to go up to the mountain. And I've looked over, and I've seen the Promised Land. I may not get there with you, but I want you to know to night that we as a people will get to the Promised Land. So I'm happy to night. I'm not worried about anything. I'm not fearing any man. Mine eyes

have seen the glory of the coming of the
Lord."

The speech was delivered on April 3, 1968 at Mason
Temple in Memphis, Tennessee.

Essay 2: Time to Move

Summary: This essay provides the justification and context for the formation of a new Black American nation. It considers contemporary conditions and explores why circumstances appear to oppose the formation of a new Black American nation. It then forecasts the conditions that are likely to unfold that will lead Black Americans to form their own new nation. Even if the aforementioned conditions do not materialize, the decision to form a new nation serves as a test for Black Americans to determine whether they are truly reliant (trust) on their Creator for guidance. It is instructive to note that the corruptible and incorruptible cannot exist side-by-side. Therefore, if Black Americans choose to be a holy nation, then they must "Wherefore come out from among them, and be ye separate, saith the Lord" (*Holy Bible, 2nd Corinthians*, 6:17). The reality is that Black Americans have now been trained in every field and are prepared to use their natural and spiritual knowledge to form a new nation that exemplifies the nature and character of those who truly love God. This essay serves as a setup for the final essay that highlights the process by which Black Americans may form their new nation.

Introduction

The first chapter of this book considered the question, "Why might the people known today as Hebrews or Jews not be the "chosen people of God?" Even if it is proven that the Jews are not the "chosen people," it does not automatically follow that Black Americans are the "chosen people" for all time. As stated in

Essay 1, different people have played special and important roles in moving the world forward throughout history. Those people have risen and fallen. What Black Americans can claim is that they have undergone a special set of experiences and have experienced a special set of circumstances that have partly "conditioned" or shaped them to perform a special role in the world today and for the current millennium. If this is true, then we contend that, in order for Black Americans to play the previously mentioned role, they must complete their preparation and then proceed to operationalize their new role in the world. In order to achieve this outcome, we believe that it is essential for the 40 plus million Black Americans (a nation within a nation) to form their own new nation. The third and final chapter of this book discusses the methods and procedures that can facilitate the formation of a new Black American nation.

This chapter discusses several important questions concerning current and future conditions of Black Americans, which impinge on their readiness and willingness to form a new nation and to play the role that has been established for them. First, we discuss certain reasons or barriers that prevent Black Americans from envisioning the need to form their own nation. Second, we discuss the economic conditions that characterize Black Americans as a sizeable dependent group in the United States (U.S.). Third, we discuss existing and future conditions that are likely to force Black Americans to face reality and to see the need to form their own nation. Finally, assuming that Black Americans ultimately decide to form their own nation, we delineate key benefits of nationhood.

Barriers to Envisioning a New Nation

On January 20, 2009, Barack Obama was sworn in as the first Black American President of the United States. Viewed as the highest political office in the land, it is easy to conclude that Black America, as represented by Mr. Obama, has "made it" in the U.S. Why would a people, who have positioned one of their own in the presidency, venture to consider forming a new nation? Moreover, many Black Americans have become superstar entertainers (sports, music, radio, television, and cinema), chief executive officers, and wealthy entrepreneurs; i.e., they have achieved the ultimate "American Dream." Clearly, these Black Americans would be averse to uprooting themselves in order to transition to a new nation where such opportunities would not be so readily available—at least initially. But even Black American politicians, who occupy seats in the U.S. Congress, state legislatures, and county and municipal governments—types of positions that would, theoretically, be available in a new nation—are also likely to have an aversion to the idea of nation formation. In fact, almost any Black American, who has worked in the system to obtain an education and has captured employment with compensation that is sufficient to facilitate the acquisition of certain assets (e.g., homes, automobiles, financial and physical capital investments, and retirement accounts), will likely reject, a priori, the idea of nation formation. The only group of Black Americans, who would likely be predisposed to nation formation, would be those Black Americans who are not plugged tightly into the system.

Because the "have nots" are the only subgroup that would appear to benefit from nation formation at this point, and because they may not have the wherewithal to move forward on this issue alone, nation formation efforts are not likely to be initiated by them. It is tragic that the "haves" possess a myopic view and do not choose to "plan for war in times of peace." The "haves" ignore the fact that they are held up high as "special cases" in order to perpetuate the idea that the American Dream remains attainable. If all non-wealthy Americans (Black, White, Asian, Hispanic, Native American) suddenly realized that the gamble for the "American Dream" is not fair, and that the proportion of Americans who achieve this dream (i.e., possessing millions or billions of dollars in assets) is quite miniscule, then the motivation and incentive to keep working to achieve the dream would disappear. Disappearance of the dream would mean disappearance of effort—would mean disappearance of America as we know it today. Black American "haves" also ignore the fact that, while they may be significantly better off than Black American "have nots," the former remain far behind White American "haves."

However, there is one fact that Black American "haves" cannot deny. Although they may have "made it," at least in the eyes of America's "have nots," they continue to face discrimination and racism by White American "haves"—many of whom represent old, traditional wealth in the country. Certain clubs and social circles remain inaccessible to Black American "haves" even with all of their wealth. These conditions have to tear at the psyche of Black American "haves." They must see, as Malcolm X once put it, that they are "Mr. and Mrs. In Between";

neither accepted by the super rich, nor comfortable with middle-class or poor Americans.[8] The Honorable Minister Louis Farrakhan quoted Muhammad Ali during his 2007 Savior's Day Address saying, "I don't care how much money you have, to them [meaning White Americans], you are still just a Nigger."

It is just a matter of time before Black American "haves" and "have nots" will find common ground and move toward nation formation. The "haves" will seek to rid themselves of the stigma that they are not good enough, even with all of their wealth, while the "have nots" will seek a place where they can contribute to the growth and development of a nation, and where they will not face the type of discrimination and racism that they face perpetually in the U.S.

Black Americans as a Dependent Group

What would the U.S. unemployment rate be if there were no Black American workers? In November of 2009, the unemployment rate stood at 10 percent.[9] This percentage is based on a total labor force of 153.9 million, with 15.4 million total unemployed workers, 2.8 million Black American unemployed workers, and 14.9 million Black employed workers. When we "do the math," (i.e., remove Black Americans from the labor force and make the jobs that they hold available to White workers), we determine that, the revised national unemployment rate would be negative (i.e., there would be a dearth of 3.2 million White workers because the number of

---

[8] This statement is taken from a speech delivered by Malcolm X (circa 1960) entitled, "The End of White World Supremacy."
[9] See Bureau of Labor Statistics, U.S. Department of Labor (2009), *The Employment Situation—November 2009.*

White unemployed was just 11.6 million workers, while Black Americans held 14.9 million jobs). This "negative" unemployment rate is far below the traditional full employment target (i.e., an unemployment rate of between four and six percent). Consequently, in this extreme case analysis, the U.S. would not be experiencing a recession if there were no Black American workers—at least theoretically. While it is not true that all unemployed non-Black American workers today are displaced by Black workers, it is true that many non-Black American workers are out of jobs because Black American workers have captured those jobs.

It is unfortunate that we cannot say that, if one removes all Black American businesses from the nation's landscape, then one would be removing a sizeable number of jobs from the American economy. The fact of the matter is that, although there were 1.2 million Black American-owned businesses in the U.S. in 2002, only 94.5 thousand or 7.8% of those businesses were large enough to support employees.[10] Many will argue that this failure of Black Americans to create business and jobs—i.e., stand on their own two feet—is wrapped up in the Willie Lynch syndrome because Black Americans have been manipulated and trained to embody a divisive mentality and to project little self-love. Others will argue that there are so few employing Black business because of racism and discrimination. We should realize, however, that non-Black Americans have no incentive to search for truthful or logical reasons for

---

[10] See Census Bureau, U.S. Department of Commerce (2006). *Black-Owned Firm: 2002.* Interestingly, the 7.8% of employing Black American-owned businesses for 2002 compares with 27.9% for 1969—the first year for which the census was taken.

this apparent failure of Black Americans to be self-supporting. In other words, many non-Black Americans are increasingly viewing Black Americans as a dependent group, which is producing adverse outcomes for the nation.

Why do non-Black Americans adopt this perspective? For many reasons. The key reasons are delineated below:

- Black Americans' high school and college graduation rates. Heckman and LaFontaine (2007) place the 2005 high school graduation rate for Whites at 83% and for Blacks at 66%.
- Black Americans' relatively poorer performance on standardized tests. The National Center for Education Statistics, U.S. Department of Education (2009) reports that, for the 2007-8 academic year, the combined critical reading and mathematics scores on the SAT for Whites averaged 1065, while it averaged just 856 for Blacks.
- The disproportionate rate at which Black Americans participate in the nation's crimes and the resultant disproportionate incarceration rate. According to a Bureau of Justice Statistics report by Sabol, West, and Cooper (2009), 3,310 Black American males and females per 100,000 Black Americans were prisoners under Federal or state jurisdiction. The comparable statistics for White Americans was 537 per 100,000.[11]

---

[11] These statistics are based on the total number of prisoners under Federal and state jurisdiction in 2008--1,540,100. However, it is important to recognize that the later estimate rises

- Black Americans' rate of substance abuse. The National Center for Health Statistics (2009) reports that 9.8% of the Black American population over the age of 12 engaged in illicit drug use during 2006. The comparable estimate for White Americans is 8.5%.
- The rate at which AIDS infections occur among Black Americans. According to the Centers for Disease Control and Prevention, U.S. Department of Health and Human Services (2009), of the 549,196 persons living with AIDS in the United States during 2007, 48% or 263.6 thousand were Black Americans. Thirty-three percent of the total was White.
- The media's history of highlighting all of the aforementioned conditions, without providing countervailing evidence of positive outcomes for Black Americans.[12]

It is important to reiterate that non-Black Americans, like most people in the world today, are engulfed in living a fast-paced existence that is accelerated by jobs that require 12-to-18 hour day or more commitments; jet airline travel; the capacity to reach out and touch others in the world 24/7 simply with a few strokes of a finger using a hand-held device; and by a 24/7 media that moves audiences quickly from one story to another interspersed with the ubiquitous commercial and with no time to come up for air in between. These busy people do not have time to consider why a subgroup within the nation cannot "get

---

to 2,304,115 when one includes prisoners held in local jails. Unfortunately, the Bureau of Justice report does not parse the 764,015 difference between the two values by race/ethnicity.

[12] See Robinson (2009), "Black Unemployment and Infotainment" for a discussion of this topic.

its act together." This unwillingness to dig deeper into the Black American condition is buttressed by the fact that non-Black Americans can look in a near spot and find at least one Black American who has excelled— even to reach the level of president of the U.S. no less. Therefore, many non-Black Americans, consciously or unconsciously, view Black Americans as a problem that they would like to wish away. They are reminded of these sentiments each time they have an opportunity to see a news story on television, in the newspaper, or on the Internet which portrays an unthinkable crime by a Black American (usually a male) against a Black or White woman or child.

Conditions that will Force Nation Formation

Believe it or not, the just-discussed sentiments are brewing in the hearts and minds of non-Black Americans. Those sentiments constitute a powder keg that is poised for an attack. A question that Black Americans should ask is, "What conditions or set of circumstances could evolve that would serve as a match for the powder keg?" A more important question to ask is, "What type of explosion will occur when the match touches the powder keg?" Let us remind you that, hate crimes against Black Americans is on the rise in the U.S.; increasing 8.0% to 2,876 during 2008 from 2007.[13] The Federal Bureau of Investigation (2009) statistics show that, where the offender was known, nearly 80% of hate crimes against Black Americans were perpetrated by White Americans. Will the explosion be characterized by an

---

[13] See *USA Today* (2009), "Hate Crimes Against Blacks, Religious groups Rise."

accelerated rate of hate crimes? Will the explosion reach the point of genocide?

The types of conditions that could serve as the "match" are mainly economic in nature. Americans are grounded in materialism. Economists have taught them that more is better: More money, more living accommodations, more means of transportation, more food, more sex, etc. When these "mores" are under the threat of reduction, Americans go looking for explanations. Each one asks, "Why should I have less? What did I do, other than act as a good American in search of the American dream? Why don't I have a job? Why are interest and inflation rates at such high levels? Why is the dollar so weak, which prevents me from purchasing the goods that I desire from abroad or from taking exotic vacations to foreign lands? Why are health insurance costs so high? Why are taxes so high?"

Some of the foregoing questions are not applicable in an extreme sense in 2009. However, let us assure you that many of these "match" questions will become pertinent in the period ahead. If the U.S. experiences a "W-shaped" or elongated recovery following the recent global financial and economic crises, matches may begin to fall out of the matchbox. After the recovery is underway, and assuming that the economy accelerates rapidly and that the dollar's weakness continues, higher rates of inflation may surface. If the Federal Reserve Board is unable to nip inflation in the bud, for whatever reasons (including an unwillingness to return the economy to a recession-like state), then it may be forced to raise interest rates to very high levels to quell inflation. On the other hand, the need to borrow to finance economic stimulus and new programs that have been undertaken by the Obama Administration may increase the risk associated with U.S. Government debt and, therefore, drive up interest rates. Higher interest rates increase the cost of production and often accompany higher inflation.

If emerging market and developing economies continue to grow at relatively brisk rates, while Western developed economies continue to experience economic weakness, then investors may turn increasingly to countries, such as China, India, Vietnam, Indonesia, Brazil, South Africa, and even Russia. Such investor behavior would place downward pressure on the dollar, making it even weaker than it is today.

The U.S. Congress is now considering healthcare reform. The stated goal is to ensure that healthcare is affordable for all Americans and that most Americans have access to healthcare. It may turn out that the plan that is adopted may achieve the stated goals. On the other hand, we must be cognizant of the adage: "When the government seeks to do you a favor, watch out." Irrespective of the type of healthcare reform that is approved, an entire set of conditions could unfold that make healthcare more expensive. As our world has become increasingly complex and technological, so has healthcare and the need for it. Today, we are facing new viruses and diseases and a reduction in the efficacy of old medicines. Given the level of pollution that is building up in the world as modernization occurs at a rapid rate, we may be on the verge of a slow breakdown of our environment, which produces even more diseases and viruses that can only be mitigated at a very high cost. Not only will individuals face higher costs of healthcare, but so will the government, which promised to control the cost of healthcare.

But rising healthcare costs is just one variable in a rising debt equation that is faced by the U.S. government. It seems logical that, in their attempt to bring the Great Satan too its knees, terrorist groups will seek to open new fronts that invite U.S. intervention. Iraq and Afghanistan are not likely to constitute the end of U.S. war efforts to eliminate terrorism. Clearly, wars are costly. Add to wars the need to keep an economy afloat for an extended period using one stimulus program after another. Economists speak of Japan's lost decades during which the national debt reached 190 percent of gross domestic product (GDP). The U.S. debt-to-GDP ratio is in the 70 percent range today. Given the unpredictable nature of our world where governments appear to be continuously blindsided by the need for new spending requirements, it is possible that U.S. government debt could continue to rise beyond the point where the Obama Administration forecasts that it will begin to recede. If these conditions unfold, then, at some point, the U.S. Government is going to have to roll back tax provisions that are designed to stimulate the economy and to raise tax rates—that is, unless the economy evolves in such a way that the Laffer Curve proves true.[14]

Thus far, the discussion has been restricted to national-level considerations. What about conditions

---

[14] The Laffer Curve is linked to Reagan Administration staffer Arthur Laffer, who used earlier analysis to postulate that Federal Government revenues might be optimized by reducing tax rates. See Wikipedia (2009), "Laffer Curve."

at the state and local government levels. It is common knowledge that the 2007-2009 recession has placed a great fiscal strain on state and local governments. Given balanced–budget requirements that most state and local governments face, the financial hardships that they have encountered have been passed on to their citizens. Imagine that, not only does the future hold unfavorable outcomes for the central government's fiscal condition, but that state and local governments also experience an extended period of fiscal hardship. Under these conditions, state and local governments, too, will be forced to raise taxes or cut services even further.

In other words, it is not too difficult to imagine a feasible scenario in which economic hardship causes non-Black Americans to become overwhelmed by adverse economic conditions that then become the matches that explode the powder keg. When the powder keg explodes, Black Americans could stand at the end of a volley of racial discriminatory acts beyond those being experienced today, and even violent acts that parallel the lynching that occurred during the late 19th century and first half of the 20th century. If conditions become extremely dire, then we could experience overt and extended violence against Black Americans in the U.S.

Some might argue that these scenarios and anticipated actions are farfetched. We respond that it is important to consider the status quo before coming to such a conclusion. The status quo is that the American system has been designed to permit a limited amount of "filtering up" of Black Americans, so that certain Black Americans achieve notoriety and earn high levels of income.[15] However, the majority of Black Americans are experiencing hard times. In fact, 25 percent of Black Americans are experiencing very hard times because they are in poverty.[16] Black Americans in the latter category are not only experiencing a hard time, they are experiencing a form of slow genocide.

Is it not reasonable to equate the following conditions to slow genocide?

- Suffering frequent and extended prison terms, which expose the prisoners to AIDS, which is ultimately returned to the Black community to accelerate and exacerbate the spread of AIDS.
- The stigma that is associated with convicted criminals, which subjects prisoners to a life of no or menial employment that, in turn, leads to distress, low self-esteem, and a life of drug and/or alcohol abuse.
- An unbalanced ratio of un-incarcerated females to males which permits males to assume multiple partners, which is not conducive to the production of wholesome home environments and well-adjusted children.
- Children who are the products of unwholesome home environments, which does not facilitate their proper moral, mental, and spiritual development. These children, in turn, repeat the cycle of low educational attainment, crime,

---

[15] See Robinson (2007), "MLK: Messianic or Satanic."
[16] See the Census Bureau (2009), *Income, Poverty and Health Insurance Coverage in the United States, 2008*, p. 15.

incarceration, drug abuse, and, quite often, early death.

We believe that it is logical to conclude that the slow genocide that is described above is an American reality. Consequently, Black Americans who wish to escape this reality must make a decision to do something different. When Black Americans realize that they cannot work and "do-good" themselves into a catch-up position with the rest of America, and when they recognize that their lives constitute the type of slow genocide state that we have described above, we believe certain Black Americans will decide that quitting America is a logical and desirable option. That decision will motivate consideration of nation formation.

Simply put, the Black American experience may be likened to that of an abused wife. An abused wife's mind is filled with reasons to remain in the relationship with her abuser. In fact, the abuser is likely to have created circumstances to make the abused wife feel as if she has no choice but to remain in the abusive relationship. However, our understanding of abusive relationships informs the following prescription: "Remove yourself from the environment in which the abuse is occurring." Psychologists, counselors, and, yes, friends will encourage an abused wife to leave the environment in which the abuse is occurring. Therefore, it seems perfectly reasonable to urge Black Americans to remove themselves from their abusive environment.

The Benefits of Nationhood

The benefits of nationhood are too many to mention here. Consequently, we will focus on what appear to be the most important or meaningful benefits that will ultimately permit Black Americans to fulfill their intended role in the world.

The first and most important benefit of establishing a Black American nation is escape from the aforementioned abusive relationship. When an abused wife escapes from an abusive environment, she is permitted an opportunity to rebuild self-esteem and self-love. She comes to recognize that she is not ordained to be a victim, but has a divine right to enjoy the fresh and sweet fruits of life—not just bitter herbs. It is the rebuilding of self-esteem and self-love that enable a formerly abused wife to pick up the pieces, reclaim her right to life, and to go on to enjoy a long and wholesome life. Similarly, Black Americans, once they leave the U.S., can begin to rebuild their self-esteem and self-love. We must keep in mind that an abusive relationship normally goes on for a few years or a few decades, at most, before it is terminated. However, in the case of Black Americans, the abusive relationship has been underway for 400 years. Therefore, it will take some time for Black Americans to fully recover. Once the recovery takes hold, however, Black Americans will be well on their way to exploiting their knowledge, skill, ability, and God-given attributes to begin to achieve great things for themselves and the world at large.

Second, after an extended period of self-analysis, self-esteem building, and learning to love one another as mothers, fathers, sisters, brothers, cousins, aunts, and uncles should, Black Americans can begin to grow well-functioning and thriving communities within their new nation. A great feature of nationhood is that citizens of the nation are expected to fill the positions of leadership, responsibility, and power. An inability to play leadership roles has been one of the most frustrating aspects of the Black American sojourn in America. In addition, because a key role of a nation state is to facilitate commerce for its citizens, Black Americans will have a free hand to exercise their entrepreneurial skills and abilities. In other words, the new nation will allow Black men to be Men and Black women to be Women; i.e., they can be the responsible parties who provide fully for the well being of the people in their charge.

Third, and very important, Black Americans can begin to play the role in the world that they have been ordained to play at this critical point in World History. Today, nations of the world have developed a broad scope and breadth of technology that enables the production of more than what is required to feed, clothe, and house all people. However, there are distributional and environmental shortcomings that are the result mainly of an overemphasis on materialism, White Supremacy, and racial/ethnic differences. Given their 400-year history of slavery, racism, and discrimination in the U.S., Black Americans, more so than any other group in world history, have been shaped and prepared to comprehend fully shortcomings in the world and how best to overcome them. Equally important, Black Americans, because of their circumstances in the U.S., have learned how to create change using the fine art of diplomacy and can use these diplomatic skills to assist nations of the world in seeing the benefits of compromise and unity. Most importantly, having been a critical ingredient in the American melting pot or tossed salad, Black Americans match well physically all people of the world and, therefore, can be the "coat of many colors" with which the world's nations can identify. These factors and connections to the world will enable Black Americans to minister to those that require ministering, teach those who require knowledge, and broker agreements among those who need to agree so that the world can enjoy the extended period of joy, peace, and prosperity that has been prophesied.

The great Black American Muslim leader, Imam W.D. Muhammad, taught that in the religious literature Black Americans represent the embodiment of Jesus. During their early period in American History, Black Americans worked miracles, helping build and provide for the nation from the ground up—just as Jesus worked physical miracles during his ministry. The U.S. Civil War and the fight over slavery represent the struggle/war between good and evil, which occupied Jesus during a critical stage of his development. The lynching, racism, and discrimination that Black Americans experienced during the latter part of the 19th and first half of the 20th century represent the trial and crucifixion of Jesus. The Black American post-Civil Rights adventure, with the "benefits" of Affirmative Action and the great expansion of physical wealth among many Black Americans, represent the burial of Black Americans in a tomb (a structure of materialism which is devoid of life). Now it is time for Black Americans to rise up out of the death of materialism and return to their father in heaven. The father is the knowledge of self and righteousness that is essential to Black (African) American character and heaven is the new land/nation that Black Americans must establish.

In the course of human history, what better role to play than to bring man back up to humanity and spirituality—from the bottomless pit of lifeless materialism and technology. To the western scientific mind, man's ideal state is to be actualized by material technology that he has created. However, the human ideal is to be actualized by engaging with other humans through love and spiritual connections. Black Americans, the soul people of the world, can achieve this outcome and save the world from death and destruction. As Aretha Franklin sang, Jesus (Black Americans) can serve as "The Light of the World." If Black Americans fulfill their role, then the world will see God's glory—how He has the authority and power to make something (a great nation) out of nothing (a people devoid of substance, who had been made empty vessels of work). We say "if" because, as always, God permits choice. However, most cultures of the world include a myth about a savior in the end time. We contend that Black Americans constitute that savior. To fulfill the savior's role, all that Black Americans have to do is have faith—enough faith to found their own new nation.

Conclusion

It is perfectly fine to complain when you are experiencing hard times. But those complaints should serve as a springboard for thought and, ultimately, for action to alleviate the difficulties. For four hundred years now, Black American have complained and fought to improve their condition. Some might argue that progress has been made. Malcolm X once asked, "If a man has a six-inch knife in your back and pulls it out three inches, is that progress?"[17] Admittedly, there has been some filtering up of Black Americans within the American economic and social structure. However, the vast majority of Black Americans exist below America's "average" (median) state—with 25 percent of Black Americans living in poverty. Is that really progress—especially considering all that Black Americans have done for the nation? It is unnecessary to delineate all of the remaining unfavorable conditions that Black Americans are experiencing today. That would constitute another round of complaining.

What we can say is that Black Americans have used so many approaches in an effort to change things: Praying, voting, marching, sitting-in, studying, working hard, campaigning, saving, investing, initiating businesses, preaching, teaching, singing, and even swinging. However, Black Americans have not used a nation formation approach. Given that all of the other approaches have not achieved their intended outcomes, it is quite logical to try a new approach. Why not try forming a new nation? In the next chapter, we provide a draft blueprint for Black Americans to use in founding their own new nation.

---

[17] This statement is taken from a famous 1964 Malcolm X speech titled, "The Ballot or the Bullet."

References

Bureau of Labor Statistics, U.S. Department of Labor. (2009). *The Employment Situation—November 2009.* Washington, DC: December 4th. Retrieved from the Internet on December 19, 2009; http://www.bls.gov/news.release/pdf/empsit.pdf.

Centers for Disease Control and Prevention, U.S. Department of Health and Human Services. (2009). *HIV AIDS Surveillance Report.* Atlanta, GA. Retrieved from the Internet on December 19, 2009; http://www.cdc.gov/hiv/topics/surveillance/resources/reports/2007report/pdf/2007SurveillanceReport.pdf.

Census Bureau, U.S. Department of Commerce. (2006) . *Black-Owned Firms: 2002.* A component of the 2002 Economic Census, Survey of Business Owners. Washington, DC: August. Retrieved from the Internet on December 19, 2009; http://www2.census.gov/econ/sbo/02/sb0200csblkt.pdf.

Census Bureau, U.S. Department of Commerce, (2009). *Income, Poverty, and Health Insurance Coverage in the United States: 2008.* Census Bureau. Washington, D.C.

Federal Bureau of Investigation. (2009). *2008 Hate Crime Statistics.* U.S. Department of Justice. Retrieved from the Internet on December 19, 2009; http://www.fbi.gov/ucr/hc2008/abouthcs.html.

Heckman, J. and P. LaFontaine. (2007) . *The American High School Graduation Rate: Trends and Levels.* The Institute for the Study of Labor (IZA); Discussion Paper No. 3216. Bonn, Germany; December. Retrieved from the Internet on December 19, 2009; http://ftp.iza.org/dp3216.pdf.

Malcolm X (El-Hajj Malik El-Shabazz). (1964). "The Ballot or the Bullet." A speech delivered in April in Detroit, Michigan; http://www.youtube.com/watch?v=CRNciryImqg.

_____. (circa 1960) . "The End of White World Supremacy." A recording of this speech was obtained from the George Mason University Library in the mid-1990s.

National Center for Education Statistics. (2009). *Digest of Education Statistics, 2008 (NCES 2009-020),* Table 141. U.S. Department of Education. Washington, DC. Retrieved from the Internet on December 19, 2009; http://nces.ed.gov/FastFacts/display.asp?id=171.

National Center for Health Statistics. (2009). *Health, United States, 2008 with Chartbook.* Centers for Disease Control and Prevention, U.S. Department of Health and Human Services. Hyattsville, MD.

Robinson, B. (2009). "Black Unemployment and Infotainment." *Economic Inquiry:* Vol. 47, No. 1; pp. 98-117.

_____ (2007). "MLK: Messianic or Satanic." BlackEconomics.org. Retrieved from the Internet on December 19, 2009; http://www.blackeconomics.org/BE&Lit/MLK.pdf.

Sabol, W., West, H., and M. Cooper. (2009). *Prisoners in 2008.* Bureau of Justice Statistics, U.S. Department of Justice. Washington, DC. Retrieved from the Internet on December 19, 2009; http://bjs.ojp.usdoj.gov/content/pub/pdf/p08.pdf.

The Holy Bible. (1973). The New Oxford Annotated Bible. (H.G. May and B.M. Metzger, Editors.) Oxford University Press. New York, NY.

USA Today. (2009). "Hate Crimes Against Blacks, Religious groups Rise." November 24th. Retrieved from the Internet on December 19, 2009; http://www.usatoday.com/news/nation/2009-11-23-hate-crimes_N.htm.

Wikipedia.com. (2009). "Laffer Curve." Retrieved from the Internet on December 19, 2009; http://en.wikipedia.org/wiki/Laffer_Curve.

Excerpt from Martin Luther King's "Drum Major Instinct" Speech

Before proceeding to Essay 3, please take a moment to listen to the following audio recording of an excerpt from Martin Luther King's "Drum Major Instinct" speech, which includes important statements about service. Please click on the following link: http://www.blackeconomics.org/Quickstart/AudioLib/MLKS.mp3.

(This recording was downloaded from YouTube.com.)

Martin Luther King said:

> "…If you want to be important, wonderful. If you want to be recognized, wonderful.   If you want to be great, wonderful. But recognize that he who is greatest among you shall be your servant.   That's a new definition of greatness. This morning, the thing that I like about it, by giving that definition of greatness, it means that everybody can be great because everybody can serve. You don't have to have a college degree to serve. You don't have to make your subject and verb agree to serve. You don't have to know about Plato and Aristotle to serve. You don't have to know Einstein's Theory of Relativity to

serve. You don't have to know the second Theory of Thermodynamics to serve. You only need a heart full of grace. A soul generated by love. And you can be that servant.."

The "Drum Major Instinct" speech was delivered on February 4, 1968 at Ebenezer Baptist Church in Atlanta, Georgia.

Essay 3: Point Zero Nation Formation

Summary: This essay provides an outline of the process by which Black Americans (Afro Descendants) may form a new nation.[18] Although the process is based, in part, on the process adopted by Jews to found their nation, it reflects novel approaches—particularly in the method suggested for economic development. It highlights the unsustainable nature of current approaches to developing and sustaining economies and proposes that the economy for the new Black American nation be founded on sustainable principles. The bottom line is that Black Americans can build a new nation that excludes factors that are detrimental to a peaceful life, that expands opportunities for service, and that increases the overall well-being of members of the new nation.

Introduction

There are only two internationally recognized displaced groups that are not linked explicitly to land to which they have a claim: e.g., the Romani people of Europe (Gypsies) and Black Americans (Afro-Descendants) in the United States. History reveals

---

[18] " Afro Descendants" is a term that was recognized recently by the United Nation's Human Rights Commission to officially represent persons of lost identity in the African Diaspora—particularly the descendants of African slaves in the Americas.

that an important goal for displaced groups is to identify a homeland and to establish a nation state. While nation formation is a very distant or nonexistent thought for most Black Americans today, a series of unique events could unfold that precipitate nation formation efforts by Black Americans.[19] Unfortunately, there are no very recent historical examples of state formation to apply under such circumstances. The most recent example of point zero nation formation by a displaced group is Jewish efforts to carve out space in the Middle East to form Israel.

A starting point for analyzing Black American nation formation is to ask, (1) "What circumstances would

---

[19] It is important to define Blackness from the outset. Historically, several criteria have been used to define Blackness in the United States (U.S.): From fractional criteria (1/4, or 1/8) to a simple "one drop rule." In this case, we believe that direct descent from a Black U.S. slave is an essential characteristic of those we refer to herein as "Black Americans." Now we must ask about the path of descent. In our view, and following a certain African tradition where lineage is transmitted through the mother, it seems appropriate that descent should be established through a female. There are two additional important points to make. First, recently, courts in the United Kingdom have overruled cultural and religious traditions in determining ethnic affiliation (see Lyall, 2009). We hold that these rulings are inappropriate and we retain a genetically-based criterion for defining who is "Black American." Simply reflecting aspects of a Black "mind" and adhering to Black "traditions" is not sufficient. Second, we discuss here the formation of a Black American nation, which does not necessarily preclude non-Blacks from inhabiting the nation once it is formed. In the final analysis, the constitution of the new nation will determine who is a citizen and who is permitted to enter the nation.

motivate Black Americans to form a separate nation?" Afterwards, one could use the Israeli experience to inquire, (2) "How has statehood been achieved, and how relevant would the Israeli experience be for Black Americans?

In his famous lecture, "The African Mind," the late historian Professor John Henrik Clarke (circa 1994) intimated that, "State formation is like running a candy store," only more complicated.[20] States organize their populations around a single-goal, yet complex process, of meeting needs for life living. That is, states organize an economy that produces required goods and services and that generates the concomitant income. Most economists—even developmental economists—are trained to apply their craft to already-existing economies. Therefore, we should ask: (3) What special methods, tools, and resources are required to initiate an economy from point zero? (4) What should be the nature of the new Black American nation's economy? (5) What would be the primary moves of the strategic game that Black Americans would encounter as they seek to establish their new nation? And (6) What are the benefits of Black American nation formation?

This economic futures essay answers the six foregoing and ancillary questions, and it may serve as a future reference for Black Americans and other groups that find it necessary to undertake point zero nation formation.

---

[20] Hear Prof. Clarke's lecture entitled "The African Mind" at the following Internet Web site; http://odeo.com/episodes/3942293.

(1) Motivating Point Zero Nation Formation

There are at least two critical aspects to the motivation of point zero nation formation. First, there is the issue of "preference formation." In other words, "Why would Black Americans prefer to abandon their position as citizens of the United States (U.S.) and pursue development of their own nation?" The second aspect of the issue is the "formation of sufficient demand."

Preference formation

A variety of conditions could evolve that motivate the formation of a preference for a Black American state. Obviously, a set of conditions that economists would be most concerned about would be the development of economic conditions that make it difficult for Black Americans to survive in the U.S. Because society does not exist in compartmentalized fashion, it is highly likely that the economic conditions just described would be accompanied by unfavorable political and/or social conditions. Consider, as a possible scenario, a severe contraction in the U.S. economy on the order of the contraction experienced during the Great Depression. Simultaneously consider that the U.S. reflects an un-synthesized, diverse population of Native Americans, Whites, Blacks (Afro Descendants), Jews, Hispanics, Arabs, Islanders, and an eclectic mix of Asians. These diverse populations would align themselves politically and otherwise to rent seek for the best possible economic outcomes within the context of the contracted economy. If the economic opportunity set becomes severely constrained, then only the best organized groups would gain access to available resources. Under dire circumstances, well-organized groups would engage in a strategic game of herding lesser organized groups into an opposition against the least organized groups. Based on a variety of factors, such as the use of information technology and the extent of political and economic organization, Black Americans are not well positioned to operate in such a strategic game. Consequently, it is highly probable that Black Americans could become marginalized in this scenario. In an extreme case, Black Americans could be physically attacked by other groups based on the perception (stereotypes) that Blacks have not contributed significantly to the well-being of the nation (viz. Black Americans' roles in crime, as a significant drain on healthcare resources due to lifestyle decisions, and the failure to benefit optimally from public educational opportunities).[21] While, *a priori*, this scenario may seem somewhat farfetched, we should remember that, in many cultures, stereotypes have served as the stimulus for attacking poorly organized "out groups" and committing genocide against them. These or similar

---

[21] It is widely believed by Black Americans that "vigilante groups" view these stereotypes as reasons to motivate hateful attitudes toward Black Americans. Further, it is believed that these groups rationalize their intent by contending that the nation spends too much to meet Black Americans' needs, while Black Americans contribute little to the nation in return. These vigilante groups could be motivated to attack Black Americans in a worst-case, severe-resource-constrained scenario.

outcomes would certainly help motivate a preference on the part of Black Americans for nation formation.

On the other hand, the simple realization of the impossibility of economic equality for Black Americans vis-à-vis their White counterparts could stimulate a desire for an independent state. In other words, under normal conditions, all Black Americans would have to outperform Whites for an extended period and the latter would have to stagnate or digress in order for Black Americans to achieve economic equality. Because the just-described conditions are not likely to occur, it is literally impossible for Black Americans to ever catch up and enjoy economic equality with Whites in America. When Black Americans awaken from the illusion, "if we simply work hard and smart, then we will achieve equality," then they will become truly disillusioned with their plight in America and are likely to seek alternative strategies for living and achieving their goals. We believe that one of those alternatives could be nation formation.

Formation of sufficient demand

In *The Logic of Collective Action*, Olson (1965) outlines the principles under which groups will perform collective action—in this case, engage in point zero nation formation. Olson concludes that group members are only willing to participate in a collective action to the extent that the benefits that accrue from an action exceed the cost of the action taken. Therefore, Black Americans who design and implement a nation formation agenda must be assured that they, or their inheritors, shall harvest the benefits of the effort. In other words, the issue of demand formation essentially boils down to a cost-benefit analysis. For completeness, it is necessary to assess the costs and benefits that are to be incurred by all Black Americans who might engage in nation formation; however, given space limitation, we will focus mainly on the costs and benefits that are to be incurred by Black American leadership.

While the election of Barack Obama to the Presidency of the United States may appear to break the ceiling on political positions, the reality is that a special set of circumstances created an exceptional opportunity for Mr. Obama. The most astute political analysts are likely to argue that a reoccurrence of such a chain of events—i.e., the election of a Black president—should not be expected with great frequency. Seeming access to the office of the presidency should not obstruct the view to the seats of real power in a nation. It is common knowledge that politicians ultimately serve at the pleasure of those who underwrite the cost of their campaigns. Therefore, the thick layer of political positions that would be created in a new nation offers only one slice of power and prestige that would be available to Black Americans who would opt to engage in a collective action to form a new nation. The prime economic opportunities that emerge in a new nation include ownership and/or control of those important private or public enterprises that provide essential services for the nation: Banking, transportation, electric power, water, food, housing, communications, entertainment, education, health, etc.

The costs associated with nation formation, at least for Black leadership that would guide the process, would likely be small. Energy would have to be expended to organize the nation formation process in an administrative sense. Assuming that it is successful, then such leadership would not lose wealth during the transition to the new nation—they could liquidate their U.S. assets and invest in assets in the new nation. The greatest costs that are likely to be incurred by this leadership would be rent-seeking costs to capture their most prized positions in the new nation.

The benefits associated with nation formation include control, power, prestige, authority, and wealth that accompany operating enterprises in the new nation. As the late Prof. Clarke (circa 1994) pointed out, the state must address the economic needs of its citizens. Founding leaders of a new Black nation would, undoubtedly, have an opportunity to control the allocation of rights to operate the aforementioned key economic spheres of life. Depending on the economic and regulatory structure that is adopted in the new nation, leaders of large enterprises may inure to themselves vast amounts of desirable amenities.

Based on this brief analysis of the costs and benefits of nation formation, it seems reasonable that existing Black American leadership would recognize the benefits of collective action to achieve this outcome—especially given the types of scenarios that were put forward as motivating nation formation. Once on track with a group of core organizers, Black American leadership could leverage the broader population for resources that could be used to stimulate interest and greater overall demand for nation formation.

(2) How Has Statehood Been Achieved – How Relevant for Black America

This section of the essay recounts the process used by the Jews to establish the nation of Israel. It also includes a discussion of how Black Americans (Afro Descendants) might view their U.S. experiences as paralleling closely the Jewish experience, and of how those parallels might motivate nation formation efforts.

Forming Israel

The experience of Jews who formed Israel may be instructive for a people seeking to establish a nation state. More recently, new nations, such as Timor Leste and the former Soviet Republics represent nation formation—but for populations that already occupied the geographical territory for which new nation states were established. The Israeli experience may be especially instructive for Black Americans because the Jewish experience reveals how a people captured a geographical area that they did not occupy immediately prior to nation formation.

Wikipedia (2009) offers a concise overview of the "History of Israel" along with key details and high-quality references. For those interested in nation formation, that history delineates six critical steps: (1) A decision by a leadership group to form a nation; (2)

obtaining agreement from authorities to move forward with nation formation, including the right to occupy a geographical territory; (3) developing an organization that initiated the process of nation operation (developing laws, rules, and guidelines, and collecting resources to finance nation formation); (4) developing affiliations with relevant international authorities; (5) constructing critical infrastructure; and (6) proclaiming the new nation state.

It took the Jews around 51 years to complete these steps; from 1897 to 1948. This effort followed a nearly five-thousand-year history during which Hebrews/Jews were intermittently associated with the land now called Israel. However, important components of the overall motivation for nation formation for the Jews was centuries of oppression, exclusion, and genocide that were directed against them.

In the late 19th century, a consensus formed among certain Jews that it was in their best interest to unite in one place. No question about it, some joined the effort because they concluded that it was aligned with religious prophecy. Others joined the effort because they viewed it not only as a method for solving discrimination and security concerns, but also as a method for increasing their prosperity. Because many Jews continue to reside outside of Israel and as citizens of other nations today, it is clear that many Jews believed that it was in their best interest to not join the nation formation effort. Many of the latter Jews sought to extend their life and wealth-building efforts wherever they were located when the call came to form the nation of Israel. Nevertheless, many of these Jewish non-citizens of Israel continue to support vigorously the Jewish cause.

Leading up to and since declaration of the State of Israel on May 14, 1948, that nation has faced numerous obstacles and attacks—military and otherwise. While the U.S. and many other Western nations have been generally supportive of Israel, there were occasions when certain Western nations attempted to block progress toward Jewish nation formation, and these nations did not support Israel during some of its most difficult challenges. Still, today, no one can dispute the reality that Jews physically occupy the territory called Israel, and that Israel is a nation that is fully recognized as a member of the international community of nations by the United Nations (U.N.).

From a Black American perspective, there are two important take-aways from the Israeli experience as consideration is given to nation formation. First, ideally, the geographical area that is sought for settlement should not be disputed territory. If it is, then, even if Black Americans occupy the land, they can be guaranteed endless confrontations with those who dispute the right to occupy the land. Second, many Black Americans are not aware that an important Black American diplomat, Ralph Bunche, played a critical role in the United Nations in helping resolve many of the issues surrounding the formation of Israel.[22] It would be poetic justice if a Jew were just as instrumental in the formation of a new Black American nation.

Black Americans Following Israel

In this section of the essay, we assess the extent to which efforts at Black American nation formation might coincide with the Israeli experience. Later, we will entertain components of the strategic game that Black Americans are likely to confront should they undertake nation formation. However, it is appropriate to understand parallels in the Jewish-Black American experience at this juncture.

One cannot visit a Black American church on Sunday mornings without hearing preachers proclaim parallels between the Black American and the Old Testament Hebrew experiences. The songs that are sung, the prayers that are prayed, and the stories that are told equate the Black American experience to the experience of the biblical Jews. Jews and Black Americans share recorded histories of a certain period of servitude in a strange land.[23] In addition, the two groups share histories of oppression, genocidal

---

[22] Ralph Bunche was also the first non-White recipient of the Nobel Peace Prize; http://nobelprize.org/nobel_prizes/peace/articles/bunche/index.html .

[23] In the case of the Jews, there is some uncertainty concerning the veracity and duration of their slavery sojourn in Egypt. See footnotes 5, 6, and 7 in Essay 1: "Hebrews/Jews and Black Americans." There is no dispute about the Black slavery sojourn in the United States.

conflicts, and discrimination. A key difference between the two groups is that recorded Jewish suffering spans a more than two thousand year Diaspora, while Black American suffering spans a little less than one-half of a millennium.

According to written histories, the Jews appear to have suffered most during their sojourn in Europe. Two important sources that chronicle Jewish experiences in Europe and in the United States are Johnson's (1987) *A History of the Jews* and Brodkin's (2000) *How Jews Became White Folks & What That Says About Race in America*. Franklin and Moss' (2000) *From Slavery to Freedom* provides an excellent account of the Black American experience beginning with the journey from Africa to the latter portion of the 20th century. Readers may augment Franklin and Moss' classic work by obtaining a vivid understanding of Black Americans' struggle for justice from Williams' (1987) graphic *Eyes on the Prize: America's Civil Rights Years, 1954-1965*.

There may be debates concerning how many millions of Jewish lives were lost over the course of history to those who hated them, and whether the Jewish loss of life is less or greater than the loss experienced by Black Americans from the Middle-Passage up to today. However, there is no argument that to lose even one life due to senseless hatred, prejudice, and discrimination is a human tragedy.

In a contemporary context, Black Americans' suffering and their abuse through discrimination cannot be explained by logical reasoning. Given their educational attainment and work experience, "Why is the Black unemployment rate twice that of the White unemployment rate?"[24] Given that Black Americans constitute less than 14% of the population, "Why do Black Americans constitute nearly 40% of the U.S. prison population?"[25] Considering a recent report by the Pew Charitable Trust on poverty and mobility, "How can we explain a persistent gap in White-Black upward economic mobility—a gap that has changed little over the past 30 years?"[26] Black Americans have superseded White Americans in the rate at which they attain education since the early 1970's; therefore, one must inquire, "Why are nearly 25% of Black Americans living in poverty, while the White poverty rate hovers at less than 9%?"[27] This is just the tip of the iceberg when it comes to assessing why Black Americans cannot seem to approach even the national averages in many socio-economic categories. For example, "Why is there such a gap in Black-White homeownership rates?" "Why aren't their more Black American chief executive officers of corporations?" Even in federal, state, and local governments, it is still not uncommon to find that Black Americans are underrepresented in a significant way when it comes to key decision-making positions. Finally, and fundamentally, we must ask, "Why has the White-Black wealth gap persisted?"

---

[24] See Robinson (2009), "Black Unemployment and Infotainment," *Economic Inquiry, Vol. 47, No. 1, pp. 98-117.*
[25] See Robinson (2007), *BlackEconomics: A Primer, pp. 82-3.*
[26] See Sharkey (2009), *Neighborhoods and the Black-White Mobility Gap*, pp. 3-4..
[27] See the Census Bureau (2009), *Income, Poverty and Health Insurance Coverage in the United States, 2008,* p. 15.

Some may argue that the overwhelming majority of Black Americans enjoy a privileged lifestyle when compared with the poor in Africa and Asia. They may point to the fact that Black Americans have a combined income of over $650 billion, and that even those in poverty have access to a social safety net that makes them significantly better off than the real poor of the world.[28] Essentially, the claim would be that poverty, pain, and suffering are relative. A logical response would be that Black Americans do not reside in Africa or Asia, but in the United States, and that the discrimination, pain, poverty, and suffering that they experience is relatively more oppressive than that experienced by poor groups in other parts of the world. Simply put, the distance from the top to the bottom is greater in the United States than in most other countries. This extended hierarchy imposes massive pressure on those at the bottom—so much so, that it may one day motivate escape and nation formation efforts.

Taking into account Black American History, the suffering that has been experienced, and the fact that effecting positive change is such a struggle—even when laws have been duly enacted to create change and impose fairness (usually without the concomitant resources for enforcement)—the following questions

---

[28] This statistic is derived from the Census Bureau (2009), *Statistical Abstract of the United States,* Table 671, and reflects 2006 results. If the $650 billion in income were treated as Black America's gross domestic product, then Black Americans would constitute the 18th largest nation in the world, just behind Turkey.

cry out for answers: "Does it not make sense for Black Americans to take under advisement a new approach to unburdening their suffering?" "Should they too, like the Jews, simply leave 'Egypt'?" At the rate progress has proceeded on civil and human rights, "How long will it take for Black Americans to achieve equality?" "Why not break the illusion that equality can be achieved in America and ensure equality by achieving it in a new Black nation?"

The foregoing discussion reveals that there are similarities between the recorded Jewish historical experience and the Black American experience. Therefore, Black Americans may be well advised to make a move to establish their own new nation in the near term, as opposed to experiencing an extended Diaspora, and then trying to reform as a nation millennia hence. In the next section of this essay, we entertain a process by which Black Americans may form their own new nation. It borrows liberally from the Jewish experience.

(3) Special Methods, Tools, and Resources for State Formation

We begin this section with highlights of key considerations/decisions that must be made concerning point zero nation formation for Black Americans (Afro Descendants). Afterwards, we assess the special methods, tools, and resources that will be required to create an economy for the new nation. We conclude this section with an analysis of Black America's wherewithal to marshal the resources required to form a nation, and by discussing prospects for achieving success.

Key Decisions for Point Zero State Formation

Figure 1 (next page) presents high-level components of a process by which Black Americans can establish their own new nation. Implementers of such a process may find it necessary to expand substantially the process and add details; however, the major components of the process are not likely to change dramatically.

First.—We begin with a decision by a leading collective to initiate nation formation efforts. As discussed earlier in this essay, probably a small group of Black Americans will become convinced that the benefits of nation formation far exceed the cost of operationalizing the effort. The idea is that this collective would petition or notify the U.S. directly, or through the United Nations, concerning the intent to form a new Black nation. In his famous "Ballot or the Bullet" speech, Malcolm X (1964), advised Black Americans to petition the U.N. to press the U.S. to end discrimination. Since that time, the U.N. formed, as part of its Committee on Human Rights, the Committee to Eliminate Racial Discrimination (CERD). Currently, the U.S. is entangled in a U.N. process to make progress in eliminating racial discrimination. The most recent correspondence from the U.N. to the U.S. makes it abundantly clear that the U.S. is not making sufficient progress on fulfilling U.N.

Figure 1

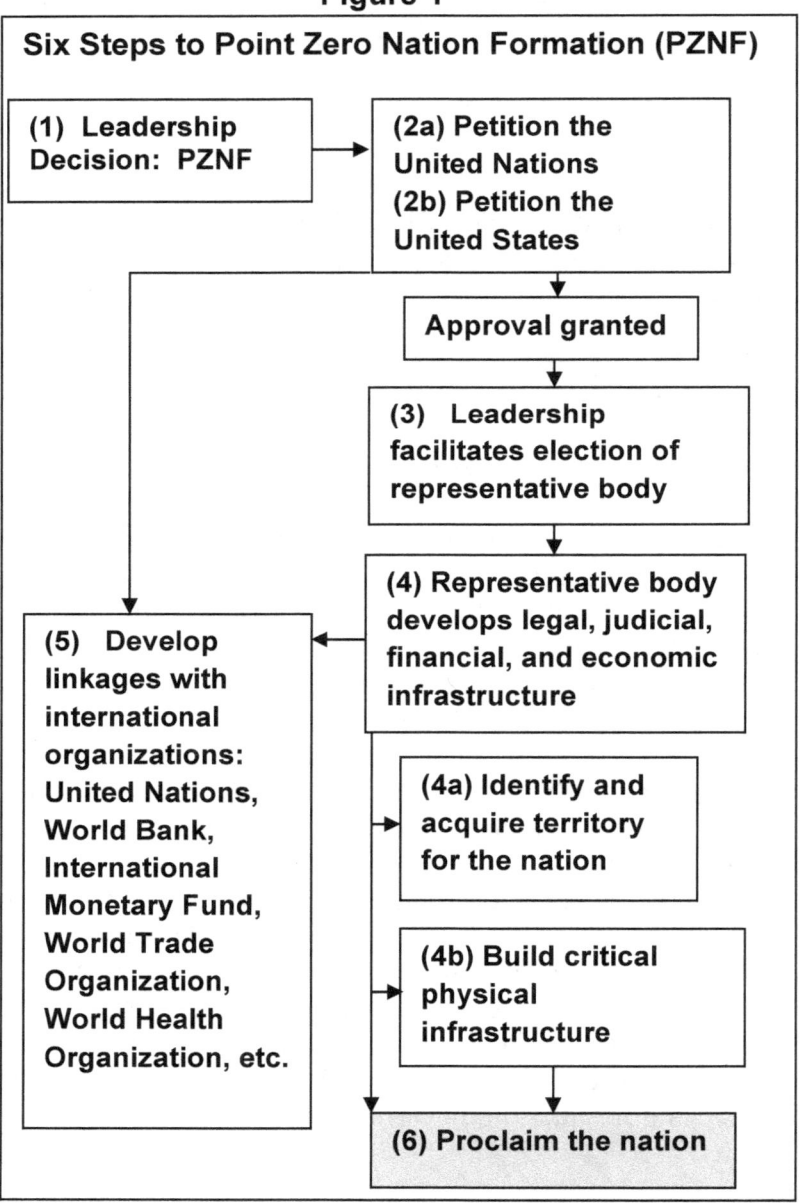

Six Steps to Point Zero Nation Formation (PZNF)

(1) Leadership Decision: PZNF

(2a) Petition the United Nations
(2b) Petition the United States

Approval granted

(3) Leadership facilitates election of representative body

(4) Representative body develops legal, judicial, financial, and economic infrastructure

(5) Develop linkages with international organizations: United Nations, World Bank, International Monetary Fund, World Trade Organization, World Health Organization, etc.

(4a) Identify and acquire territory for the nation

(4b) Build critical physical infrastructure

(6) Proclaim the nation

recommendations to end racial discrimination.[29] Our expectation is that insufficient progress will be made in the future such that conditions will evolve, which will motivate Black Americans to initiate a nation formation effort. For the sake of this analysis and without attempting to elaborate on the strategic game that will unfold when the above-mentioned petition is filed, let us assume that the U.N., the U.S., and the Black American collective leadership will reach an agreement on nation formation; i.e., approval is granted for the leadership collective to proceed.

Second.--The leadership collective must facilitate the election of a broad and representative body of Black Americans to participate in the decision making processes that will be required to complete the nation formation effort. The U.S. electoral system could be used to elect Black American representatives. For example, U.S. congressional elections could be used to elect Black American representatives to serve as shepherds of the nation formation effort. Such elections should not be problematic because our assumption is that the U.S. would have offered its support for the nation formation effort. Alternatively, depending on the state of technology, the leadership

---

[29] See a September 28, 2009 letter from the U.N.'s High Commissioner for Human Rights on the CERD's response to a U.S. response concerning recommendation to eliminate racial discrimination; http://www.aclu.org/intlhumanrights/racialjustice/41258res20090 928.html. For the U.S. correspondence, which precipitated the U.N. response, see a January 13, 2009 letter to the U.N. from the George H.W. Bush Administration; http://www.state.gov/documents/organization/113905.pdf.

collective could use a cybernetic governance process to facilitate nation formation decision making.[30,31]

Third.—The representative body should proceed to develop the legal, judicial, financial, and economic (finance and commerce) infrastructure that are required to operate a nation. It seems reasonable that the representative body could initiate the development of a constitution, which could be validated by a vote of those Black Americans who voluntarily opt into the nation formation effort. That constitution could establish the governance framework for the nation. In addition, given that the U.S. Government would support nation formation, the

---

[30] For an explanation of how cybernetic governance might work, see Robinson (2005), "Judges, the Supreme Court and Cybernetic Governance"; http://www.nationalcenter.org/P21NVRobinsonCyber1005.html.

[31] It is important to inject the following points. Many Black Americans are accustomed to being part of a strong leadership culture. This is expressed most prevalently in a religious context where Black ministers/pastors provide strong leadership for the entire church community—to the extent of playing the role of a type of tribal chief. In addition, Black Americans are very religious—with strong and complex belief systems (see Sahgal and Smith, 2009). Given these two phenomena, it may be logical for the governance framework that is established for the new nation to reflect theocratic principles. Iran is the best known theocratic society in the world today, and it is not generally viewed favorably in the Western world. Nevertheless, it may still be beneficial for Black Americans to adopt theocratic governing principles—at least as a starting point when they form their new nation. Two important final points are: (1) The biblical Hebrews only began to encounter problems when they abandoned their theocratic governance system; and (2) theocracy and democracy can coexist—they are not mutually exclusive.

representative body should seek to utilize the U.S. tax system to collect funds from Americans interested in contributing to the nation formation process. Logistically and otherwise, it seems fairly simple to establish a "check-off" on tax returns that would permit prospective citizens of the new nation (and others) to allocate a portion of their taxes due (if the U.S. Government agrees) and of their tax refunds to the representative body's treasury. That treasury would be used to manage the nation formation process; including administration, land acquisition, and physical infrastructure development. Again, given the state of technology, the representative body may use cybernetic governance to permit more comprehensive participation in these aspects of nation formation decision-making by prospective citizens of the new nation.

Fourth.--The representative body would undertake two broad tasks. (4a) First, and its most important and possibly the most difficult task, the representative body would identify and acquire the geographic territory that the new Black nation will occupy. Given that nation formation is likely to only occur at some point in the distant future, it is not useful to elaborate too extensively on the options or alternatives nor the process that could be used to complete this task. However, let us consider four areas that have been floated historically as sites for a new Black American nation and attempt to highlight the practicality of settling on one of the areas. However, before considering the four areas, let us consider how much land might be required. Consider Table 1:

Table 1.—Countries, Populations, and Land Areas

Line No.	Countries	Populations (millions)	Land Area (million square kilometers)
1.	Algeria	35.9	2.4
2.	Kenya	36.5	0.6
3.	Poland	38.1	0.3
4.	Sudan	40.1	2.4
5.	Argentina	40.5	2.7
6.	Tanzania	41.3	0.9
7.	Ukraine	45.2	0.6

Source: CIA World Fact Book (2009)

According to the U.S. Census Bureau's *Statistical Abstract of the United States*, the Black American population was about 40 million in 2009. Therefore, we considered nations with populations of 35-to-45 million when considering how much land area might be required to accommodate the Black American population. Obviously, more is better, especially if the geographical area is fertile and has plentiful water and other resources. However, based on the data provided in Table 1, we conclude that, if nation formation were to proceed in the near term, land area ranging from 0.3-to-2.7 million square kilometers would be required to accommodate the nation. With this information in mind, now let us consider the four areas that have been mentioned as possible locations for a new Black nation.

- We are probably all familiar with the 19th century effort to create a new Black nation in

Africa by the American Colonization Society.[32] What we know is that the shear distance from the U.S. to the African Continent generated a major barrier to massive migration and nation formation. Moreover, the history of Liberia does not bode well for the prospect of a smooth integration of Black Americans into Africa as a new and separate nation. Consequently, we set aside, for now, Africa as a location for a new Black nation.

- The Honorable Elijah Muhammad, a key founder and leader of the Nation of Islam (NOI) organization, inferred in his writings (Muhammad, 1965) that Black Americans should create their own new nation in the southern region of the United States. At this time, it is not certain that NOI scholars developed a detailed-enough plan for such nation formation that specifies the geographical areas that would be subsumed in the new nation. Although there has a been a significant reverse migration of Black Americans from the northern region to the southern region of the U.S. over the past two decades, Black Americans still constitute the majority population in only 77 southern counties.[33] In other words, efforts to form a Black nation in the southern part of the U.S.

---

[32] See Yarema (2006), *The American Colonization Society: An Avenue to Freedom?*

[33] See Census Bureau (2009), "Census Bureau Releases State and County Data Depicting Nation's Population Ahead of the 2010 Census." There are over 3,100 counties in the U.S.

would require that massive numbers of White Americans relocate. What we know from the India-Pakistan Partition experience is that such a process engenders a great deal of animosity. Consequently, it is probably not logical to expect the U.S. Government to agree to permit Black Americans to form their new nation in the southern part of the U.S. Moreover, scientists would probably advise against such an effort, given that global warming and climate change are expected by many scientists to render that area significantly warmer and dryer than it is today as we move forward through the 21st century and beyond.[34]

- Another prospective area for Black American nation formation in the U.S. is the far western part of the country in the states of Nevada, Utah, Wyoming, and Oregon, where the U.S. Bureau of Land Management has oversight over millions of square kilometers of grazing and other types of land. Using Bureau of Land Management's (2009) *Public Land Statistics 2008,* we determined that the previously mentioned states include a total of 0.43 million square kilometers (105.2 million acres) of public lands. This land exceeds the minimum amount required (0.3 million square kilometers) to accommodate a population of about 40 million. Although the land is not perfectly contiguous, it should be possible to

---

[34] See Karl *et al* (2009), *Global Climate Change Impacts in the United States.*

gerrymander lines around the territory to form a contiguous territory of land that could be set aside for a new Black nation (See Annexure I). Most importantly, scientists (Karl *et al,* 2009) are a bit more optimistic about future climatic conditions in the area spanned by these four states than for southern states.

- Scientists (Karl *et al,* 2009) are predicting that temperatures will rise in the northern latitudes as we proceed through the current century; i.e., even the northern regions of Canada may become more inhabitable weather-wise. Annexure II is a map from Canada's Centre for Cadastral Management (2009) and it indicates that Canada has large tracts of land (the Yukon Territory (0.5 million square kilometers), the Northwest Territory (1.4 million square kilometers), and Nunavut (2.0 million square kilometers)) that exceed the 0.3 million square kilometer land requirement for accommodating the current Black American population should these lands prove to be comfortably inhabitable in the future.[35] Therefore, Black Americans, who escaped to freedom in Canada before the Civil War, might consider securing land from the Government of Canada to accommodate their new nation. Black Americans might use the good services of the U.S. Government to help negotiate such an agreement with

---

[35] The map was obtained from Doug Culham, Deputy Survey General of Canada, via e-mail message on November 10, 2009; 613-995-2604; Doug.Culham@NRCan-RNCan.gc.ca.

Canada, and/or the representative body may negotiate its own deal with Canada. It is important to make two further notes about Canada. First, Blacks who fought with the British during the Revolutionary War were transported to Nova Scotia after the war; therefore, there is a significant settlement of Black American in Nova Scotia to this day. In addition, Canada's major cities include small, yet significant, populations of Blacks who have roots in the Caribbean, Africa, and the U.S. Second, if one removes the "d" and adds an "n" to Canada, one arrives at "Canaan"; the promised land for the Hebrews after departing Egypt. Consequently, at "d" (the) "n" (end) of their sojourn in America (Egypt), Black Americans could transition to their promised land, Canaan.

While it is not necessary to narrow the choice of prospective territories for the new Black nation at this point, the foregoing analysis reveals that the latter two options appear to offer the two best opportunities at this time. However, by the time nation formation efforts get underway, it is very possible that circumstances may have changed sufficiently to usher up new and more promising prospects.

As the representative body considers land requirements and attempts to negotiate accordingly, they should not forget an apparent commitment by the U.S. Government to award all Black males of a certain age "40 acres and mule." Of course, history reveals that a formal law to this effect was never passed by the U.S. Congress.[36]   However, considering the historical appreciation of the land values that could have been awarded at the end of slavery, or simply updating the idea to 21st century terms (say 40 acres for each Black American family today), we arrive at the amount of resources or actual land that is sufficient to accommodate a new Black nation. We should not overlook the possibility that the U.S. Government may be so heavily indebted at some point in the future that it may be predisposed to selling land to Black Americans.

We cannot close on land acquisition without re-emphasizing that the representative body must make no decision that will place the new nation in a land area that is contested. The Israeli experience vis-à-vis the Palestinians is a living nightmare. It must be possible to identify land for the new nation the occupation of which does not raise the ire of any group in the area, and/or for which clear, reasonable, and fully-agreed-upon compensation can be paid that will eliminate any prospect for later reneging or contestation.

(4b) Second, given the acquisition of land to accommodate the new nation, the representative body can commence to establish critical physical and institutional infrastructure. Physically, it may be necessary to construct certain public utility (water,

---

[36] The U.S. Congress failed to pass the Freedmen's Bureau Act in 1866, which would have permanently awarded Freedmen parcels of abandoned land following the Civil War. (See Freeman (2009); *What About My 40 Acres and a Mule?*)

electric power, and waste), governance, financial, commercial, health, and educational facilities before citizens flood to the new nation. Clearly, the new nation's planners must consider this issue and organize a development process that accommodates the flow of citizens to the nation.[37]

Fifth.—The representative body would begin to coordinate efforts to form linkages/affiliations between the new Black nation and key international organization; e.g., the U.N., the World Health Organization (WHO), the World Trade Organization (WTO), etc. Creating these linkages and affiliations usually involves elaborate, but manageable, accession processes.

Sixth.--Having accomplished the foregoing five steps, the new nation state can be proclaimed. As noted at the beginning of this essay, nation formation efforts may consume several decades. However, there will be great joy on that day when the new Black nation is proclaimed. That day shall be more joyous to the extent that the process used to birth the nation is an orderly one, and to the extent that there are no conflicts or other major problems on the horizon as the new nation arises.

---

[37] The leadership collective might consider developing a multiphase plan for inhabiting the new nation. That is, a lottery could be used to assign families dates and locations within the new nation to which they would migrate. New inhabitants could be trained to participate in the construction and development of their own new towns and cities. The phases could span a generation; thereby, providing an orderly process for developing an inhabiting the new nation.

Special Economic Methods, Tools, and Resources for Nation Formation

Clearly, Black American nation formation is an economic event. Therefore, economists will be integrally involved in the nation formation effort. However, participating economists must bring a unique set of skills to the table if they are to be successful. Unlike economists who apply their trade in the context of an existing nation state with an existing economy (i.e., a mix of human capital, physical capital, natural resources, industries, and financial resources, etc.), economists who are to help build a new Black nation must construct an economy from the ground up. It is not that the economic tools must be different; on the contrary, economic principles can be applied ubiquitously. What must be different is the mentality and flexibility of the economists who engage in the task. They may best be characterized as interdisciplinary economists who have wide-ranging knowledge, skills, and abilities (KSAs). To the extent that a sufficient pool of economists with such characteristics cannot be identified, then it will be necessary to assemble a team of economists, other social scientists, and physical scientists who can build the new nation effectively. All of this may be transparent to certain readers, but we thought it necessary to emphasize the point because it is a point that is easily overlooked. Below, we highlight nine important KSAs that economists would be well served to possess when they undertake point zero nation formation.

1. They must be multidisciplinary in nature— not just economists, but psychologists, political scientists, futurists, engineers, lawyers, entrepreneurs, historians, sociologists, environmentalists, etc. They must reflect an architect's, not a social engineer's mentality.

2. They must bring a full complement of social science tools to the task in order to be able to assess the human capital and natural resources that are to be available in the nation so as to determine where comparative advantages might exist.

3. They must decide from the outset the mix of goods and services that should be produced as opposed to selecting thrust industries as is often the case when planning for a developing economy. For national security purposes, there is a need to be self-sufficient in the production of certain goods and services. Such goods and services must be produced in the nation, with remaining goods and services requirements being imported.

4. They will require the services of specialized experts (e.g., geologists to catalogue natural resource reserves), and they must adhere to the opinions of these experts.
5. They must bring financial, management, and budgetary skills to the task in order to assess how to invest initial resources for optimal returns and to develop budgets that are reasonable and that do not dig a deep hole for the new born nation.
6. They are likely to require micro-financing expertise in order to assist new entrepreneurs in forming businesses.
7. They must possess human resource and advertising skills in order to attract the highest qualified human capital possible to implement the plans and programs that are formulated.
8. They must employ media judiciously and expertly in order to guide the new nation toward optimal outcomes, and to share appropriate attitudes that will facilitate the best possible state formation.
9. Above all, they must be excellent time managers in order to schedule developments so that key components of the economy are in place as they are required: e.g., transportation infrastructure; water, electric power, and solid waste

utilities; governance systems and facilities; health services, educational services; etc.

Obviously, this list could be expanded; however, it reflects the essential point that economists' requirements for nation building are quite different from economist requirements for nation maintenance and growth.

Building the economy of the new nation is akin to building the great temple in Jerusalem. Consequently, the economists who undertake the task must have the acumen, special skills, and divine-like practices reflected by the great Hiram Abiff who labored effortlessly to finish the temple for King Solomon.[38]

Do Black Americans have What it Takes to Form a Nation?

Throughout their history in the U.S., Black Americans have served in essentially all occupations—even president of the nation. Therefore, there should be no occupations that are required in the new nation that cannot be filled by existing Black American talent. However, one fact remains true: For 2008, the 15.9 million Black American employed workers concentrated themselves into only twelve detailed occupational groupings (Offices workers-9.9%, Sales-

---

[38] See *The Holy Bible* (1971), I King 7:13-14 and II Chronicles 2:13.

8.3%, Cleaning service workers-5.0%, Educators-4.6%, Food service workers-4.5%, Management-4.3%, Transportation workers-3.4%, Health workers-3.2%, Production workers-3.2%, Personal care services-3.2%, Social service workers-2.4%, and Protective service workers-2.3%).[39] These data reveal that almost 54% of the Black American labor force falls into these twelve occupational groups. If this trend continues, there may be shortages within certain occupational groups when nation formation commences. Below we will discuss methods for addressing labor shortages as part of the broader economic development effort; nevertheless, efforts should be made to prevent shortages from occurring. Therefore, when asked whether Black Americans have what it takes to form a nation, the answer is a resounding yes. However, it is important to caveat that answer with a cautionary note that takes into account the fact that Black America need to begin to redistribute its labor force more broadly across key industries (especially science and technology industries) in the economy. In addition, even in industries where Black Americans have concentrated themselves, there is a need to ensure that there is a sufficient vertical distribution; i.e., it is important that Black Americans achieve sufficient representation along the leadership hierarchy and not be distributed mainly horizontally at the bottom of the industry

---

[39] These shares were derived from Table 11, "Employed persons by detailed occupation, sex, race, and Hispanic or Latino ethnicity" from the 2008 *Current Population Survey*, which is conducted by the Census Bureau, U.S. Department of Commerce on behalf of the U.S. Department of Labor, Bureau of Labor Statistics.

pyramid. On the other hand, one could argue that a nation of 40 million is small and cannot be expected to operate a full scope and breadth of industries. Therefore, the new Black nation may achieve success by focusing on those industries for which expertise exists and outsource the remaining production requirements—at least initially. In case a particular industry is of great strategic importance and little expertise is available within the nation, then the nation would be wise to build that expertise by ensuring that high quality members of its population receive training in order to operate in that industry prior to nation formation.

What are the Prospects for Success?

It turns out that inquiring about prospects for successful nation formation by Black Americans is not a relevant question. The fact of the matter is that once the nation is established, then there is no turning back. The relevant question to pose is, "What will be the quality of life in the new nation?" Nations of the world represent an extended hierarchy of living standards: From the abject poverty of Myanmar and portions of India, to comfortable lifestyles that exist in Taiwan, South Korea, and Argentina, to the elevated quality of life that can be found in Japan and the Western European nations. It is logical to conclude that Black Americans, with their high level of education, skill set, and wealth, should be able to build a nation that provides a relatively high quality of life for its citizens within a reasonable period of time. While there is no question that, like every other nation, the new nation will encounter serious challenges during and after formation, by no means should we expect that nation to ultimately reflect the type of very difficult living conditions that we find in the poorest of African, Asian, and Caribbean nations. On the other hand, even in the poorest nations of the world, there is a type of pride inherent in the citizens that is difficult to find even among fairly well-off Black U.S. citizens. Once Black Americans form their own new nation—and as long as they are willing to meet the initial challenges of nation formation with patience—it is just a matter of time before pride will form and they will be willing to expend the energy and make the types of sacrifices that will produce a nation with a high-quality living standard that others will seek to emulate and clamor to enter.

(4) The Nature of the New Black Nation's Economy

Point zero nation formation is likely to be successful to the extent that an economy is developed with the characteristics that are to be discussed below. It is reasonable to suggest that the economy for a new Black nation should also be new. History reveals that the three primary Western economic systems have flaws: Capitalism, Socialism, and Communism. Given that conditions have changed markedly since these three systems were first envisioned, it is possible to envision a new economic system that builds on currently available concepts and technologies. We suggest that a new Black nation build an economy based on Neo-Utilitarianism.

In its simplest form, traditional utilitarianism has been described as "the greatest good for the greatest number of people." We adhere to this idea but suggest an economy that is based on a new utilitarianism that focuses on "service."

In a religious context, man was made to "serve his creator." Black American slaves were taught and forced to serve their masters. As a deeply religious people with a history of slavery, Black Americans know best how to serve. We therefore promulgate here the idea of developing an economy that features service, that de-emphasizes materialism, and that emphasizes spiritual determinism.

How would this economy work? The economy would be based on *laisez-faire* principles, but it would entail guarantees of life's essential requirements: Food, clothing, and shelter.[40] However, economic agents would be required to work. The important difference between work in the new Black nation versus work in most other economies is that economic agents would be urged to train for, and to adopt, occupations in which they have the highest autonomous interest. By "autonomous interest" is meant that individuals would not form a job preference based on the level of compensation or on a glamour factor, but on their innate preference for the work. If one is naturally motivated each day to work because it is the job for

---

[40] In other words, the economy would be modeled on freedom of action, but with guarantees. Related restrictions will be discussed below.

which one has the highest innate preference, then the highest performance and utility should result.

The economy should be based on the principle of providing extended choices, as opposed to the principle that underlay Western economies; i.e., a closed system with limited choices. We should take heed of a conclusion that can be drawn about the quality of life in the Western world. It is perfectly rational to argue that an African bushman has a higher quality of life because he has several choices when he arises each day: e.g., till his small garden; fish from a local stream; visit a friend in a nearby village; devote time to making a needed repair; simply relax; etc. Westerners, on the other hand, have only one choice; go to work because their entire livelihood is tied to a job that produces income, which makes possible all other facets of their life. Failure to go to work places their very existence in jeopardy.

We promote a natural/sustainable neo-utilitarianism. Here we define natural/sustainable to mean that all aspects of the economy should be designed to have a minimal effect on the surrounding creation.[41] An

---

[41] In our view, "sustainable" means that, if one is inserted into an environment, then that one should take no action to upset the pre-existing balance if the environment is to retain its original character. *Homo Sapiens* have adopted a completely different attitude about their environment—choosing to impose maximum impact on their environment, with little attention to the detrimental effects of their actions; viz., pollution and greenhouse gases and their resultant creation of global warming and sea-level rise. In other words, it is now possible to fulfill Hayek's

economy based on the essential nature of an Amish or Kibbutz-type framework should not be overlooked. No technology should be adopted that destroys without purpose. Further, adopted technologies should minimize waste.

Economists in the new nation should use available, nondestructive technologies to collect economic statistics for analytical purposes. Therefore, a central authority would have sufficient information to estimate accurately the demand and supply of required goods and services.[42] Wages and salaries would be determined according to a standard; deviations from this standard would be incorporated only to increase or reduce the supply of labor to those occupations that reflect shortages or surpluses. Periodically, standardized compensation would be recalibrated so that inter-occupational compensational differences would be minimized—to the extent possible.

The economy would emphasize uniformity. What we know is that homogeneity produces acceptance of a

---

(1948) requirements for the efficient and effective use of knowledge in society.

[42]An assertion that the idea of a centrally controlling authority may sound communistic or socialistic in nature is correct. Admittedly, these two economic systems have been criticized for their inability to use information effectively in order to manage an economy successfully. However, the 21st century brings with it an endowment of high performance computers and micro-scanner data, which can be used to manage an economy successfully. That is, sufficient information can be obtained about the workings of an economy to set appropriate prices—the signal that enables rational economic agents to make optimizing choices.

more even distribution of income in a society (Robinson 2002). That is, societies that are the most ethnically homogenous reflect the most evenly distributed incomes. An even distribution of income can facilitate faster economic growth and development (Bénabou, 1996). The other key element that can help facilitate an efficiently functioning economy is a more even distribution of assets (Deininger and Squire, 1997). Therefore, we strongly suggest that a mechanism be fashioned that permits the even distribution of the land that is to be occupied by the new Black American nation. It would be anachronistic for the new Black nation to reflect the same types of land and wealth concentrations that are commonplace in poorly functioning economies around the world. Of course, the nation should permit the transfer of land so that each citizen can transact with owned assets to optimize utility.

As growth occurs, wealth is created. In the neo-utilitarian economy that could be established in a new Black nation, wealth should be utilized to serve the overall society. When we see great wealth in creation, we can determine that it does not serve individuals, but is permitted to form for the greater good.[43] On the other hand, when great wealth is reserved for a few, nature finds a way to challenge or

---

[43] For example, the wealth of water that forms the great oceans, lakes, and rivers serve to house the great schools of fish and sea animals. The great tropical forests and stands of timber house great biodiversity and operate as carbon sinks, and they produce immense volumes of fresh air, respectively--both for the overall good of the planet.

eliminate it.[44] We propose that the central authority of the new economy manage the redistribution process in the new Black nation by calling for periodic jubilees (*Leviticus* 25:8-17, *Holy Bible*, 1971). Such jubilees could be used to redistribute wealth and provide a new beginning for everyone in the society.[45] Just as periodic relocations give economic agents a fresh start, jubilees can be used to accomplish the same outcome.

One might argue that economic agents in the new Black nation would vote with their feet if there were restrictions on wealth accumulation. A logical response is that such action would be contingent upon the philosophical perspective of the agents. If the society teaches the value of community, sharing,

---

[44] For example, when a few agents have access to vast resources, other agents begin to infringe on the territory to initiate a redistribution of wealth. We see this in many open areas where what may begin as a few animals occupying a territory being transformed overtime so that more animals come into the territory to automatically redistribute the wealth of resources that are available. The redistribution occurs until equilibrium is achieved. On the other hand, in some cases, too many animals arrive in a territory, which then creates a shortage of resources. Ultimately, however, through contestation or starvation, equilibrium is restored over time.

[45] In the old civilizations of Pagan, Myanmar (a.k.a. Burma), the society incorporated a natural process of purging wealth. A heavily religious society (Buddhist), the cycle would begin with royalty owning much and the *sangha* (priestly community) and peasants owning little. However, royalty would purge its sins by distributing wealth to the *sangha* to build temples. The *sangha* would hire peasants to build the temples. When royalty found its wealth dwindling, then it would impose taxes to accumulate wealth again. Afterwards, the cycle would begin anew.

service, and working for the greater good (i.e., utilitarianism and spiritual determinism), then it is possible that economic agents would not depart the society as long as the quality of life is satisfactory.[46]

An additional important feature of the proposed neo-utilitarian economy for the new Black nation is conscription. While it is suggested that the new Black nation not build a military defense force, it is suggested that citizens of a certain age undergo conscription for a certain period. The major tasks of the conscripts would include building or developing projects that reflect market failures. The central authority would be warranted in intervening in the economy to ensure that such projects are completed.[47] In addition, conscripts would be used to provide temporary labor to industries that reflect shortages. These assignments would be temporary; i.e., until adjustments to the wage and salary structure attracts new supplies of labor.

(5) Nation Formation's Strategic Games

When Black Americans (Afro Descendants) decide to undertake nation formation, there are likely to be internal (to the Black American population) and

---

[46] It may be sufficient to argue that wealth is not always a source of happiness, nor a panacea for creating the good life.

[47] For example, the North Korean Government practices periodic mobilization of focused or broad sectors of its population to achieve policy objectives: Building roads, schools, mines, etc. In the new Black nation's case, the mobilization would be restricted to the conscript population.

external forces at play to thwart the effort. Which reasons will surface for and against nation formation? Which roadblocks will be raised to prevent or hamper the process? How should Black Americans, who are intent on completing the process, react to these barriers to success?

As always, based on the "Willie Lynch" principle, divisive techniques will be employed by external forces to attempt to prevent nation formation.[48] That is, external forces will seek to exploit differences between members of the Black American population and seek to highlight why those differences are sufficient to prevent the new Black nation from being successful. The leadership of the nation formation process must anticipate these ploys and inoculate the Black American population against Willie Lynch tactics beforehand. The bottom line is that, according to Williams (1987), Black people of the world have historically achieved great success in managing states. Numerous African nations serve as examples of successful Black states today. To the extent that recent and current Black states experience difficulty, it is due, in part, to the fact that they manage their states using Western principles and their operations are contaminated by a European mindset. It is critical that leaders of the nation formation effort research and study the historical principles of nation formation and operation that have existed in a Black and Asian

---

[48] In his October 1995 Million Man March Address, the Honorable Minister Louis Farrakhan discussed an historical personality, Willie Lynch, and the principles that the latter designed to create division and distrust within the Black slave population during the 18th Century.

context in order to observe and implement principles that will guarantee long-term success.

One key component of a successful nation formation strategy is to prevent preoccupation with materialism, excess, and growth. Man and woman can only wear one outfit of clothes at a time, live in one room at a time, and eat one meal at a time. If the nation can provide the outfits, rooms, and meals as they are needed, then that is a successful state. The idea that success must be defined by surplus is antithetical to the normal principles of nature; i.e., surplus is a sign of imbalance and is usually corrected in nature by a natural process. Therefore, the new Black nation should be based on a new set of principles and must be evaluated by a new set of standards.

Simply put, Black Americans must be willing to shed their current properties and to travel to a new land in order to build a new society from the ground up. Arguments against making this effort will be mainly, "Why should I give up all that I have built, in order to go and rebuild." The answer is: "Because it is in Black America's long-term best interest to do so." If Black Americans remain in the U.S., then they will be absorbed or destroyed.[49] On the other hand, if they

---

[49] Simply put, and as noted in *The Holy Bible* and *Holy Qur'an*, conditions in the United States can be interpreted to imply that the nation has adopted a policy of stifling or killing young Black males and retaining Black females. Under these circumstances, it is impossible for Black Americans to survive as a people. If it is critical for Black Americans to survive as a people, then the only method for achieving this outcome is to form a new nation.

form a new nation, then they are likely to survive for the millennia ahead.

Formally, an internal strategic game may be modeled as a type of prisoner's dilemma game. The two sets of players in the game are Black American "Haves" and "Have Nots" in the context of the U.S. experience.[50] They have two choices: "Remain in the U.S." or "Form a new nation." We have developed payoffs for the game and present them in Figure 2 (next page). The first value in each cell represents the payoff for "Have Nots," while the second value is for "Haves".

We see that a "Have Nots" strategy of remaining in the U.S. will produce payoffs of 2 and 1 if "Haves" choose to "remain in the U.S." or "form a new nation," respectively (first column). However, a "Have Nots" strategy of form a new nation will produce payoffs of 3 and 4 if "Haves" decide to "Remain in U.S." or "Form a new nation," respectively (second column). The related payoffs for "Haves" are straight forward (by rows). The payoffs convey the fact that both "Have Nots" and "Haves" are unambiguously better off if they adopt a dominant "Form a new nation" strategy, as opposed to "Remain in U.S." However, if "Haves" decide to remain in the U.S., then the payoffs for "Have Nots" are higher if the latter proceeds with

---

[50] By "haves" we mean Black Americans who possess above the median levels of education, income, and wealth; by "have nots" we mean Black Americans who possess lower than the median levels of education, income, and wealth—especially those that live in poverty.

Figure 2
Black "Have Nots" in the U.S.

		Remain in U.S.	Form a new nation
Black "Haves" in the U.S.	Remain in U.S.	2,5	3,4
	Form a new nation	1,6	4,7

nation formation. In identical fashion, "Haves" should proceed with nation formation whether "Have Nots" choose to participate in the process or not. In other words, the Nash equilibrium is for both groups to adopt a "Form a new nation" strategy.

The payoffs in this prisoner's dilemma-type game can be manipulated to convey different stories. However, the payoffs presented here imply the following two key conclusions: (1) It may be possible for either group to pursue nation formation separately and to derive benefits, but a joint nation formation effort will produce the best outcome; and (2) if the two groups adopt opposite strategies, then a penalty is imposed on the group that decides to remain in the U.S. These conclusions are logical in the sense that a unified force is likely to produce a better outcome than a fragmented effort.

Once Black Americans clear the hurdle of deciding to pursue nation formation, they will face the prospect of engaging in a multi-play game with the U.S. This game may be modeled as an "extensive" game. We prepared such a game, and present it below in Figure 3.

Figure 3

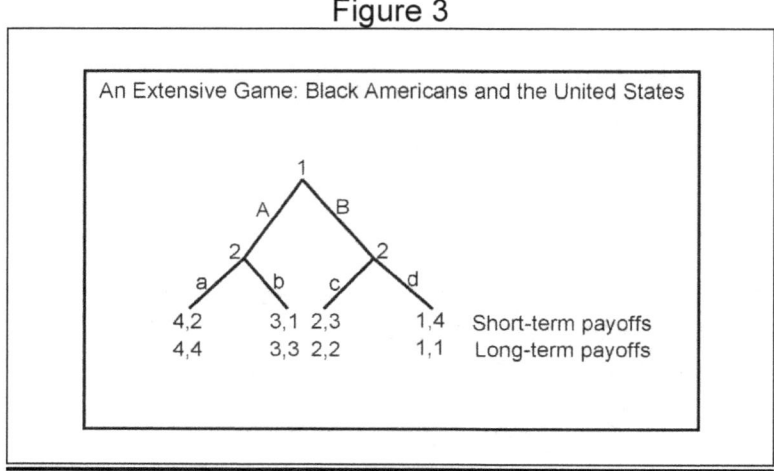

An Extensive Game: Black Americans and the United States

4,2	3,1	2,3	1,4	Short-term payoffs
4,4	3,3	2,2	1,1	Long-term payoffs

Players 1 (Black Americans) and 2 (the U.S. Government) each have a turn in this extensive, multi-play game. Our assumptions are:

- Player 1 can form a new nation, with or without the cooperation of Player 2
- Player 1's efforts to form a new nation will be viewed favorably by other nations and international organizations
- Player 1 can impose a cost on Player 2 if the latter does not cooperate with the former's efforts

- Other nations and international organizations will view unfavorably Player 2's actions to block Player 1's actions

There are both short-term and long-term payoffs to the strategies that are adopted. The first row of payoffs at the bottom of Figure 3 are short-term payoffs, while the second row represents long-term payoffs. The first payoff values are for Player 1 and the second payoff values are for Player 2.

In this game, Player 1 plays first and opts to form a new nation (A) or remain in the U.S. (B). Player 2 follows with the following actions: If Player 1 moves to form a new nation, then Player 2 can cooperate (a) or block the effort (b); and if Player 1 opts to remain in the U.S., then Player 2 can make concerted efforts to improve conditions for Player 1 (c), or maintain the status quo (d).

In the short run, Player 1's unambiguous optimal strategy is to form a new nation. For Player 2, however, the optimal strategy is to cooperate with Player 1 under a form a new nation option, and to maintain the status quo if Player 1 opts to remain in the U.S. In the long term, the unambiguous optimal decision is for Player 1 to form a new nation and for Player 2 to cooperate with Player 1.

Again, the payoffs in this extensive game may be manipulated to test various choices or strategies. However, we have presented logical assumptions, basic choices and strategies, and reasonable payoffs for this game in order to portray the type of strategic game that will likely be encountered with external forces once a decision is made to form a new Black American nation.

Assuming that Black Americans will ultimately make a decision to embark upon a nation formation effort, that they will be able plan a nation formation process and execute it successful, and assuming that they will be able to successfully win strategic and extensive games that they will face *en route* to nation formation, let us now consider the benefits of forming a new Black American nation.

(6) Benefits of a New Black American Nation

The ultimate goal of mankind is oneness/unity. In the Christian tradition, there is the idea of the oneness of God and the brotherhood of man. In the Islamic tradition, there is the idea that God permitted division among men only as a test of man's ability to reclaim unity. So why further disaggregate the world by forming a new nation for Black Americans (Afro Descendants)? In fact, it is for the sake of unity that a Black nation must be formed. Just as it may be necessary to "dive to rise," in this case, it is necessary to "divide to unify." The reasoning is as follows:

- First, Black Americans have been molded into shape as a very special group of people. As a result of Black American suffering, this rainbow of the world is a most empathetic people. Black Americans, more so than any other group of people, understand what it means to sacrifice for others, to cooperate, and to make peace in the world. It is certainly true that, today, Blacks murder each other senselessly as a result of their sickness, frustration, and ignorance, but seldom do they kill members of other ethnic groups. They have a very high regard for others' lives, and they help protect others' lives; viz. Blacks' outstanding service as police officers and as members of the U.S. military. They defer to others, even to their own detriment. This type of personality or mind is sorely needed in a world of cold and cruel materialism in order to transition it back toward warm humaneness. Once a more humane mentality is established, the world has an excellent possibility of achieving unity and oneness. It is that unity and oneness that will permit the world to solve its critical problems.

- Second, if Black Americans do not establish a new nation, then this empathetic, loving, and deferring personality will be lost to the world. Those Black Americans who attain middle-class-and-above status will fade into the American melting pot, never to be heard from again. Black Americans who languish in poverty will be destroyed by crime, imprisonment, drug use, poverty, and disease. The sum total of this outcome is the absence of the healing balm that the world so direly needs to find its way back to unity/oneness.

- Third, when a new Black American nation is formed, despite any difficulties that might be visited upon that formation, the people that populate that nation will embody the type of love, peace, and empathy described above.

The new nation will permit this rainbow of people to heal themselves psychologically and physically and grow into maturity. It is this rejuvenated and strong Black man and woman, descendants of the founders of civilization, who can promulgate a powerful injection of love, peace, and empathy to the world that will enable a coming together of the world in peace, and love, and harmony that is required. Such a strong Black nation is required to save the world, make it one, and set the stage for problem resolution that will establish a new framework for living for mankind on planet earth in the millennia ahead. It is this Black nation that can help the world return to the point of high civility such that even the languages that are spoken will no longer require a word for "jail."

(7) Conclusion

This essay has provided a methodical analysis of the intricate maze that is nation formation for a people who are not linked to an independent government or territory on a pre-existing basis. Few stones have gone unturned as we discussed how efforts might be initiated to found a new nation; reviewed Israel's history as a prototype for nation formation; analyzed the methods, tools, and resources that are required to build a nation; divined the economy for the new nation; prepared prospective nation builders for the strategic games that they will confront; and revealed the world-saving benefits of the new Black American nation.

This is not to say that a complete and perfect plan is embodied in this essay. What we have here is a solid starting point for refinement. Now it is up to those who will form this new nation to take this essay, tear it apart, and reassemble it to meet the specific requirements of the day when it will be time to "walk into Jerusalem."

At this writing, we are anticipating that there will be an elongated period of contemplation about this very important topic and action. However, each day, there is new evidence that the United States is increasingly hamstrung by previous excesses and current limitations. The situation could deteriorate more rapidly than we anticipate and the nation formation effort may have to be undertaken on a sooner-than-expected basis. Therefore, we hope that many will read this essay now and begin the thought process that will produce workable revisions that make the nation formation process even more straight-forward, efficient, and effective.

We believe that some Black American collective will take ownership of these ideas and begin to plan earnestly for their eventual and certain implementation.

(8) References

Bénabou, R. (1996). "Inequality and Growth." NBER Working Paper Series 5658. National Bureau of Economic Research. Cambridge, MA.

Brodkin, K. (2000). *How Jews Became White Folks & What That Says About Race in America.* Rutgers University Press. New Brunswick, NJ.

Bureau of Labor Statistics, U.S. Department of Labor, (2009). "Employed Persons by Detailed Occupation, Sex, Race, and Hispanic or Latino Ethnicity;" *Current Population Survey.* Washington, DC: (ftp://ftp.bls.gov/pub/special.requests/lf/aat11.txt.) .

Census Bureau, U.S. Department of Commerce. (2009). "Census Bureau Releases State and County Data Depicting Nation's Population Ahead of the 2010 Census." Washington, D.C.: May 14; (http://www.census.gov/Press-Release/www/releases/archives/population/013734.html).

Census Bureau, U.S. Department of Commerce, (2009). *Income, Poverty, and Health Insurance Coverage in the United States: 2008.* Census Bureau. Washington, D.C.

Census Bureau. U.S. Department of Commerce. (2009). *Statistical Abstract of the United States.* U.S. Department of Commerce, Census Bureau. Washington, D.C. (http://www.census.gov/compendia/statab/).

Centre for Cadastral Management. (2009). "Canada Lands." Canada's Department of Natural Resources. Ottawa, Canada.

Clarke, J. (circa 1994). *The African Mind.* An audio recording of this lecture by Prof. Clarke is available at the following Internet Web site; (http://odeo.com/episodes/3942293-John-Henrik-Clarke-The-African-Mind).

Deininger, K. and L. Squire. (1997). "Economic Growth and Income Inequality: Reexamining the Links." *Finance & Development.* International Monetary Fund. Washington, D.C. March; pp. 38-41.

Franklin, J. and A. Moss, (2000). *From Slavery to Freedom.* Alfred A. Knopf. New York, NY.

Freeman, G. (2009). *What About My 40 Acres and a Mule?* Yale New Haven Teacher Institute; (http://www.yale.edu/ynhti/curriculum/units/1994/4/94.04.01.x.html).

Hayek, F. (1948). "The Use of Knowledge in Society." *Individualism and Economic 'Order.* The University of Chicago Press. Chicago, IL; pp. 77-91.

Johnson, P. (1987). *A History of the Jews.* HaperPerennial. New York, NY.

Karl, T., Mellilo, J. and T. Peterson (editors). (2009). *Global Climate Change Impacts in the United States.* Cambridge University Press. Cambridge, MA.

Lyall, S. (2009). "Who is a Jew? Court Ruling in Britain Raises Questions." The New York Times. November 7th; (http://www.nytimes.com/2009/11/08/world/europe/08 britain.html).

Olson, M. (1965). *The Logic of Collective Action*. Harvard University Press. Cambridge, MA.

Osborne, M. (2006). Strategic and Extensive Games. Department of Economics. University of Toronto. Toronto, CA; (http://repec.economics.utoronto.ca/files/tecipa-231-1.pdf).

Malcolm X (El-Hajj Malik El-Shabazz). "The Ballot or the Bullet." A speech delivered in April 1964 in Detroit, Michigan; (http://www.youtube.com/watch?v=CRNciryImqg).

Muhammad, E. (1965). *Message to the Black Man in America.* Secretarius MEMPS Ministries Publications. Phoenix, AZ.

National Science and Technology Center, Bureau of Land Management. (2009). "BLM Public Lands and Administrative Jurisdictions." U.S. Department of the Interior; (http://www.blm.gov/nstc/jurisdictions/index.html).

Robinson, B. (2002). "Income Inequality and Ethnicity: An International Perspective." A working paper presented at the 2002 International Association for Research on Income and Wealth in Djuronaset, Sweden; (http://blackeconomics.org/BE&Lit/IncomeInequalityandEthnicity.pdf).

_____. (2005). "Judges, the Supreme Court, and Cybernetic Governance." National Center for Public Policy Research, Project 21. Washington, D.C.; (http://www.nationalcenter.org/P21NVRobinsonCyber1005.html).

_____. (2007). *Black Economics: A Primer*. BlackEconomics.org. McLean, VA; (http://www.blackeconomics.org/BEAP/BEFD.pdf).

_____. (2009). "Black Unemployment and Infotainment." *Economic Inquiry*. Vol. 47, No. 1; pp. 98-117.

Sahgal, N. and G. Smith. (2009). *A Religious Portrait of African-Americans*. Pew Forum. Washington, D.C. (http://pewforum.org/docs/?DocID=389#a).

Sharkey, P. (2009). *Neighborhoods and the Black-White Mobility Gap*. Economic Mobility Project. Pew Charitable Trust. Washington, D.C.

The Holy Bible. (1973). The New Oxford Annotated Bible. (H.G. May and B.M. Metzger, Editors.) Oxford University Press. New York, NY.

The Holy Qur'an.(1410 (1988/9)). English Translation of the Meaning and Commentary by Mushaf Al-Madinah An-Nabawiyah. King Fahd *Holy Qur'an* Printing Complex. Al-Madinah Al-Munawarah, Saudi Arabia.

Wikipedia. (2009). *History of Israel;* (http://en.wikipedia.org/wiki/History_of_Israel).

Williams, C. (1987). *The Destruction of Black Civilization: Great Issues of A Race from 4500 B.C. to 2000 A.D.* Third World Press. Chicago, IL.

Williams, J. (1987). *Eyes on the Prize: America's Civil Rights Years, 1954-1965.* Penguin Books. New York, NY.

Yarema, Allan (2006). *The American Colonization Society: An Avenue to Freedom?* University Press of America, Inc. Lanham, MD.

Annexure I

Bureau of Land Management Maps of Nevada, Utah, Wyoming, and Oregon

Source: National Science and Technology Center, Bureau of Land Management. (2009).

The maps are gray scale. Please visit the following Internet Web site to view these maps in color: (http://www.blm.gov/nstc/jurisdictions/index.html).

Nevada

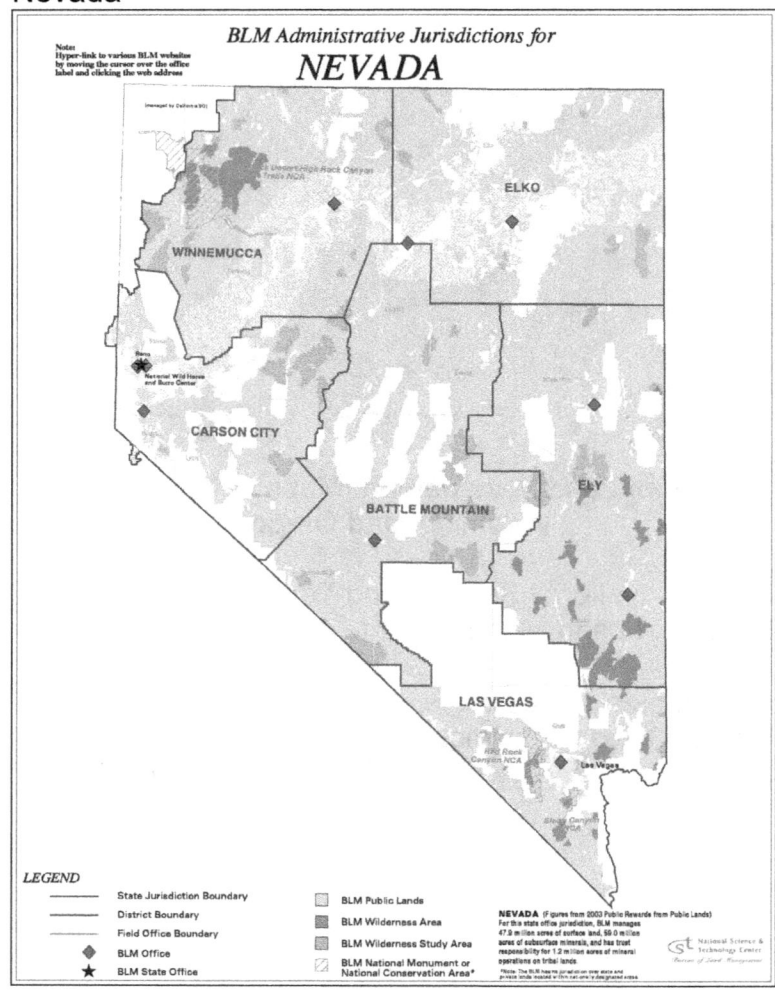

Utah

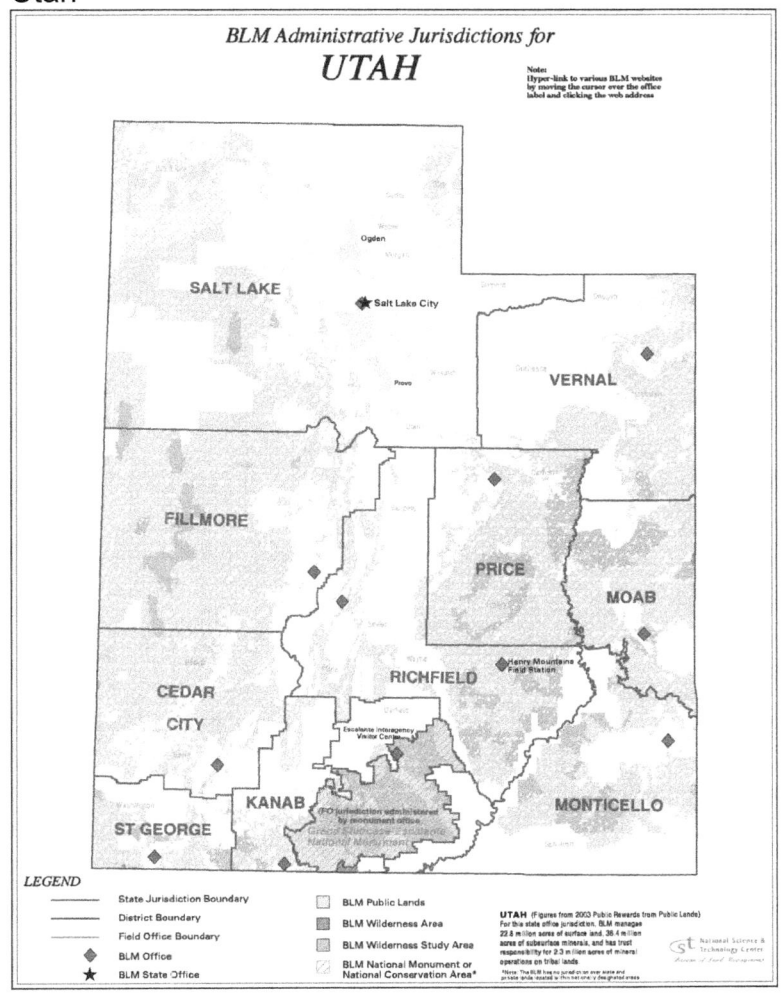

Wyoming

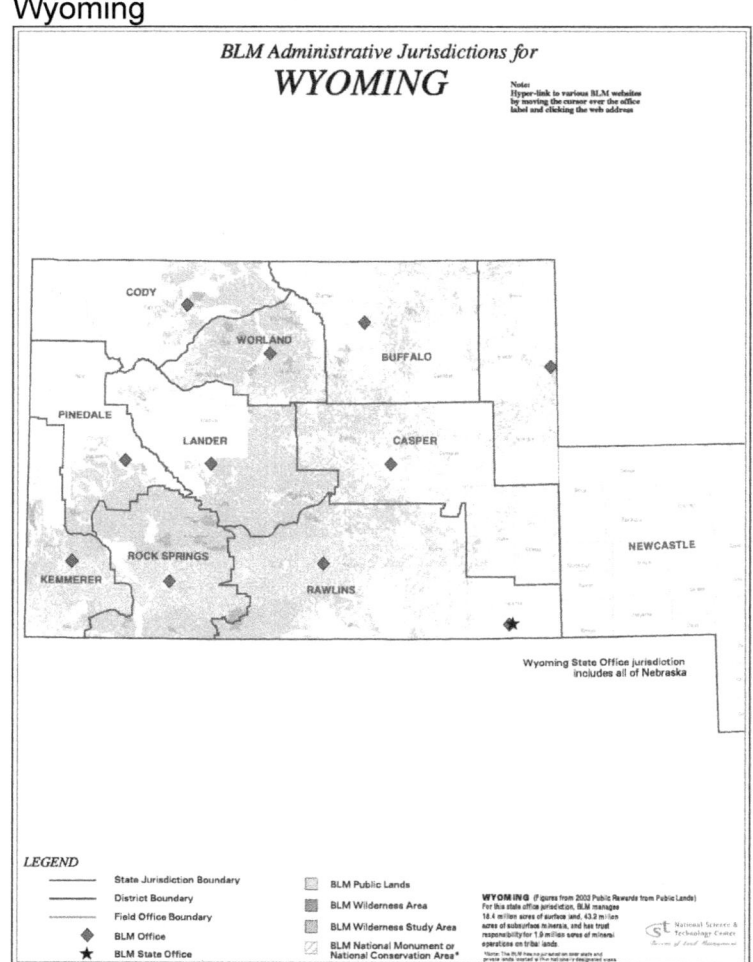

Oregon

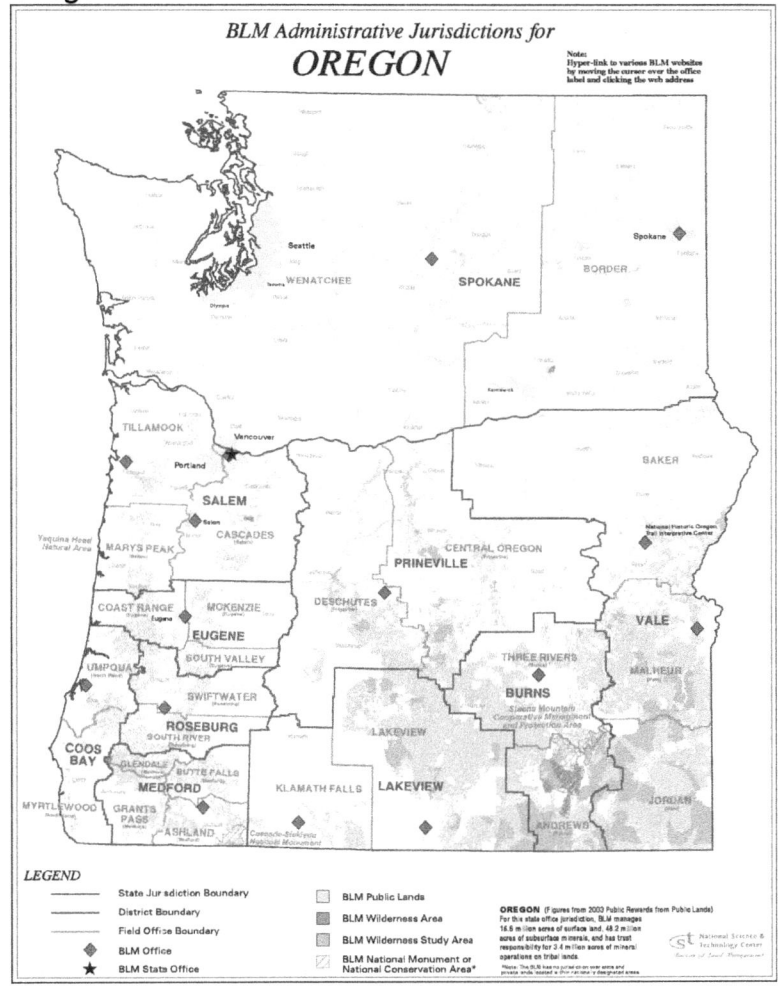

Annexure II

Map of Canada

Source: Centre for Cadastral Management, Canada's
Department of Natural Resources

The map is gray scale. To obtain a color rendering of
this map, please contact the Centre for Cadastral
Management; call 613-995-2604 or write to
Doug.Culham@NRCan-RNCan.gc.ca.
. . . . .

Canadian Lands

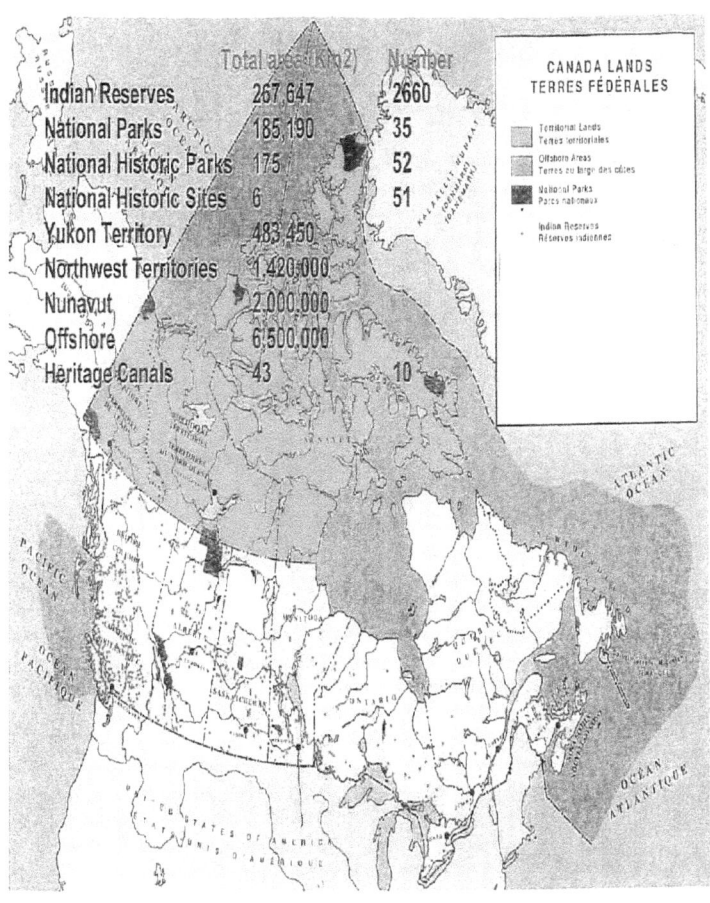

	Total area (Km2)	Number
Indian Reserves	267,647	2660
National Parks	185,190	35
National Historic Parks	175	52
National Historic Sites	6	51
Yukon Territory	483,450	
Northwest Territories	1,420,000	
Nunavut	2,000,000	
Offshore	6,500,000	
Heritage Canals	43	10

CANADA LANDS
TERRES FÉDÉRALES

Territorial Lands
Terres Territoriales

Offshore Areas
Terres au large des côtes

National Parks
Parcs nationaux

Indian Reserves
Réserves indiennes

CHOSEN

BBR:122509

www.ingramcontent.com/pod-product-compliance
Lightning Source LLC
Chambersburg PA
CBHW072200280526
45788CB00002B/809